BY THE EDITORS OF CONSUMER GUIDE®

LOW CALORIE
MICROWAVE
COOKBOOK

BEEKMAN HOUSE
New York

CONTENTS

Printed and bound in Yugoslavia
by CGP Delo

Library of Congress Catalog Card Number:

This edition published by:
Beekman House
Distributed by Crown Publishers, Inc.
225 Park Avenue South
New York, New York 10003

ISBN: 0-517-61662-9

On the front cover: Burgers with Mushroom Sauce, Crunchy Asparagus and Peach Melba
On the back cover: Ginger Peach Parfait

HOW TO USE THIS BOOK

If you are on a diet or just interested in eating light, this cookbook will offer nutritious, easy-to-prepare recipes.

Microwaving foods retains nutrients, requires little fat and enhances flavor. Sensible eating becomes easier with the speed of cooking in a microwave; leftovers are also suited to microwaving because food doesn't dry out or lose flavor when reheated.

The following information will further explain how to get the most out of each recipe.

Nutritional information, including a per-serving measurement of calories, sodium and cholesterol content, are given with each recipe. All ingredients listed as optional are included in this measurement. Use this data to help you select foods which are best for your personal diet.

If you have special dietary needs, plan a weight loss program by consulting your doctor or dietitian.

SERVING SIZE

Controlling food quantity is important when you're interested in eating light. Each recipe lists a typical and adequate serving size. If you eat more or less, you will need to adjust the nutritional data accordingly.

CALORIES

The amount of calories a person needs is determined by activity level, size and age. Artificial sweeteners cannot give uniform results, so they have not been used within the recipes. In some cases, minimal amounts of high calorie foods, such as margarine, have been included for flavor.

LOW SODIUM

Sodium levels for each recipe are calculated using all listed ingredients. To further reduce sodium, omit salt and use a salt substitute, light soy sauce, or low-salt bouillon and catsup. The most common source of sodium is table salt (1 teaspoon equals 2,132 mg. of sodium).

LOW CHOLESTEROL

The per-serving cholesterol measurement is based on all listed ingredients, using polyunsaturated margarine and oils.

APPETIZERS & BEVERAGES

CLAM DIP

½ pkg. (4 oz.) Neufchâtel
   cheese
1 can (6½ oz.) minced clams,
   drained
¼ cup plain low-fat yogurt
¼ cup chopped onion
1 teaspoon snipped fresh
   parsley
1 teaspoon prepared
   horseradish
1 teaspoon Worcestershire
   sauce
  Paprika

Serves 10
Serving size: 2 tablespoons

Place cheese in small baking dish. Microwave at 50% (Medium) 45 seconds to 1¼ minutes, stirring after half the time. Stir in remaining ingredients. Microwave at 50% (Medium) 3½ to 5½ minutes, or until heated through, stirring after half the cooking time. Sprinkle with paprika.

Serve hot or cold with assorted fresh vegetables.

Per Serving:
Calories: 56
Sodium: 16 mg.
Cholesterol: 9 mg.

CRAB-STUFFED CHERRY TOMATOES

1 pint cherry tomatoes
1 can (5 oz.) crab meat,
   rinsed and drained,
   cartilage removed
2 green onions, finely
   chopped
1 teaspoon white wine vinegar
¼ cup finely chopped green
   pepper
½ teaspoon parsley flakes
¼ teaspoon dill weed
⅛ teaspoon white pepper
2 tablespoons seasoned dry
   bread crumbs
  Paprika

Serves 5
Serving size: 5 tomatoes

Cut stem end from tomatoes and scoop out pulp. Set aside. Combine remaining ingredients except paprika in small mixing bowl. Stuff tomatoes with crab mixture. Place tomatoes on paper towel-lined plate, with small tomatoes toward center. Microwave at High 2 to 4 minutes, or until heated through, rotating plate once or twice. Sprinkle with paprika.

NOTE: For low sodium diets, substitute well-drained frozen crab meat.

Per Serving:
Calories: 80
Sodium: 282 mg.
Cholesterol: 16 mg.

MARINATED VEGETABLES ▶

1 cup tomato juice
½ cup water
½ cup thinly sliced celery
1 teaspoon onion powder
½ teaspoon basil leaves
½ teaspoon oregano leaves
¼ teaspoon garlic powder
⅛ teaspoon pepper
⅛ teaspoon tarragon leaves
1 cup cauliflowerets
1 cup broccoli flowerets
1 cup thin carrot strips

Serves 8

Combine tomato juice, water, celery, onion powder, basil, oregano, garlic powder, pepper and tarragon in 2-qt. casserole. Microwave at High 3 to 5 minutes, or until bubbly.

Stir in vegetables. Microwave at High 3 minutes. Reduce power to 50% (Medium). Microwave 3 to 5 minutes, or until flavors are blended and vegetables are softened. Serve warm or chilled, as desired.

NOTE: for low sodium diet, use low-sodium tomato juice.

Per Serving:
Calories: 23
Sodium: 65 mg.
Cholesterol: 0

◀ GINGERED MEATBALLS

Meatballs:
1 lb. extra lean ground beef
3 green onions, chopped
1 egg, slightly beaten
1 teaspoon ground ginger
⅛ teaspoon garlic powder

Sauce:
½ cup water
2 teaspoons cornstarch
1 tablespoon soy sauce
1 teaspoon white wine vinegar
2 teaspoons parsley flakes
   Dash hot red pepper sauce

Serves 12
Serving size: 3 meatballs

Combine meatball ingredients in medium mixing bowl. Blend thoroughly. Form meatballs using 2 level teaspoons of meat for each. Place meatballs in 12 × 8-in. baking dish. Microwave at High 4 to 7 minutes, or until meatballs are no longer pink, turning once or twice during cooking. Remove meatballs from dish. Set aside.

Combine water and cornstarch in 1-cup measure. Blend into meat juices in baking dish; add soy sauce, vinegar, parsley flakes and hot red pepper sauce. Microwave at High 4 to 7 minutes, or until thickened and bubbly, stirring once or twice. Pour sauce over meatballs. Microwave at High 1 to 3 minutes, or until mixture is heated through.

Per Serving:
   Calories: 60
   Sodium: 103 mg.
   Cholesterol: 43 mg.

SPICY SHRIMP

1 pkg. (10 oz.) frozen medium
   size cleaned shrimp,
   defrosted, rinsed, drained
¼ cup white wine
1 clove garlic, pressed or
   minced
½ teaspoon parsley flakes
⅛ teaspoon salt, optional
⅛ teaspoon black pepper
⅛ teaspoon tarragon leaves
⅛ teaspoon thyme leaves
   Dash red pepper flakes
1 small bay leaf

Serves 5

Combine all ingredients in 2-qt. casserole. Cover with wax paper. Microwave at High 3½ to 6 minutes, or until shrimp are opaque, stirring after half the time. Let stand 3 to 5 minutes.

Per Serving:
   Calories: 114
   Sodium: 96 mg.
   Cholesterol: 85 mg.

STUFFED CELERY

 2 tablespoons assorted dry
     vegetable flakes
½ teaspoon onion flakes
½ teaspoon freeze-dried chives
 3 tablespoons water
 2 oz. Neufchâtel cheese
 4 large celery stalks,
     ends trimmed
   Paprika

Serves 10
Serving size: 2 pieces

In 1-cup measure combine vegetable flakes, onion flakes, chives and water. Cover with plastic wrap. Microwave at High 20 to 45 seconds, or until vegetable flakes are soft. Set aside.

Place cheese in small bowl. Reduce power to 50% (Medium). Microwave 20 to 45 seconds, or until softened. Stir in vegetable flakes.

Stuff celery with cheese mixture. Cut each stalk into 5 pieces. Sprinkle with paprika.

Per Serving:
  Calories: 18
  Sodium: 1 mg.
  Cholesterol: 1 mg.

SWEET & SOUR CHICKEN WINGS

 2 lbs. chicken wings
¼ cup white wine vinegar
 1 tablespoon honey
 1 tablespoon soy sauce
 1 tablespoon catsup
½ teaspoon ginger
 1 can (8 oz.) chunk pineapple,
     packed in own juice
½ teaspoon bouquet sauce
⅛ teaspoon lemon-pepper
     seasoning

Serves 12
Serving size: 2 wings

Cut chicken wings into 3 pieces, separating at joints. Discard wing tips. Combine remaining ingredients and wing pieces in plastic bag or small bowl. Refrigerate overnight, turning wings once or twice. Place marinade and chicken wings in 8×8-in. dish. Cover with wax paper. Microwave at High 8 to 12 minutes, or until chicken wings are fork tender, stirring once during cooking.

NOTE: for low sodium diet substitute low-salt soy sauce and catsup.

Per Serving:
  Calories: 71
  Sodium: 105 mg.
  Cholesterol: 58 mg.

SPICED TOMATO COCKTAIL

1 cup water
1 teaspoon instant beef
   bouillon granules
3 to 4 drops hot red pepper
   sauce
½ teaspoon summer savory
   leaves
2 cups tomato juice
⅛ teaspoon garlic powder
¼ teaspoon onion powder
   Celery stalk or green onion

Serves 6
Serving size: ½ cup

Combine all ingredients except
celery in 2-qt. casserole. Cover.
Microwave at High 5 to 10
minutes, or until boiling. Garnish
with celery stalk or green onion.

NOTE: for low sodium diet
substitute low-salt bouillon and
tomato juice.

Per Serving:
Calories: 16
Sodium: 481 mg.
Cholesterol: 0

FRESH CRANBERRY JUICE ▲

1 lb. cranberries
2 slices orange
6 cups hot water
¼ cup fructose

Serves 12
Serving size: ½ cup

In 5-qt. casserole combine cranberries, orange slices and water.
Cover. Microwave at High 20 to
25 minutes, or until cranberries
split. Strain. Stir in fructose and
chill. Serve mixed with orange
juice or use in Citrus Warmer,
page 13.

Per Serving:
Calories: 27
Sodium: 0
Cholesterol: 0

◄ SPICED COFFEE

4 cups hot water
1 stick cinnamon
1 teaspoon whole allspice
½ teaspoon vanilla
1 tablespoon sugar
⅛ teaspoon nutmeg
1 tablespoon instant coffee
  Lemon twists or cinnamon
  sticks, optional

Serves 4
Serving size: 1 cup

Combine water, 1 stick cinnamon, allspice, vanilla, sugar and nutmeg in 2-qt. mixing bowl. Microwave at High 6 to 8 minutes, or until mixture comes to a full, rolling boil. Immediately remove from oven; strain. Pour mixture over instant coffee in a serving pot. Stir to dissolve.

If desired, serve with a twist of lemon or a cinnamon stick.

Per Serving:
  Calories: 8
  Sodium: 0
  Cholesterol: 0

SPICED TEA

4 cups hot water
1 tablespoon grated orange
  peel
1 teaspoon grated lemon peel
4 whole cloves
1 stick cinnamon
3 tea bags

Serves 4
Serving size: 1 cup

In 2-qt. casserole combine water, orange peel, lemon peel and spices. Cover. Microwave at High 6 to 10 minutes, or until boiling. Remove from oven; immediately add tea bags and let steep 3 to 5 minutes. Serve hot or chilled.

Per Serving:
  Calories: 0
  Sodium: 0
  Cholesterol: 0

CITRUS WARMER

2 cups unsweetened orange
  juice
1 cup water
1 cup Fresh Cranberry Juice
  page 11
½ cup pineapple juice
1 tablespoon lemon juice
3 to 4 drops red food coloring
¼ teaspoon ground coriander
  Mint leaves

Serves 8
Serving size: ½ cup

In 2-qt. casserole combine the liquids and coriander; cover. Microwave at High 10 to 12 minutes, or until boiling. Reduce power to 50% (Medium). Simmer 5 minutes. Serve hot, garnished with fresh mint leaves.

Per Serving:
  Calories: 24
  Sodium: 0
  Cholesterol: 0

16

ROAST TENDERLOIN

¼ teaspoon garlic powder
¼ teaspoon onion powder
¼ teaspoon lemon pepper
　Dash cayenne
2 lb. beef tenderloin roast

Serves 8

Combine garlic and onion powders, lemon-pepper and cayenne. Rub well over surface of roast. Place tenderloin on roasting rack in 12 × 8-in. baking dish. Shield ends and 1 inch down sides of tenderloin with aluminum foil. Microwave at High 3 minutes. Reduce power to 50% (Medium). Microwave 5 minutes. Turn roast over and rotate dish; remove shielding. Microwave at 50% (Medium) 8 to 12 minutes longer, or until internal temperature reaches 125°. (Roast will be medium rare). Let stand, tented loosely with foil, 10 minutes. Temperature will rise 15° to 20°.

Per Serving:
Calories:　　165
Sodium:　　94 mg.
Cholesterol:　77 mg.

FLANK & TOMATO CURRY

1 to 1½ lbs. flank steak, thinly
　sliced
½ cup thinly sliced celery
¼ cup chopped onion
¼ cup chopped green pepper
1 tablespoon cornstarch
1 can (16 oz.) whole tomatoes,
　drained, juice reserved
1 teaspoon curry powder
1 tablespoon parsley flakes
1 teaspoon salt, optional
¼ teaspoon pepper

Serves 6

In 2-qt. casserole combine flank steak, celery, onion and green pepper. Microwave at High 7 to 11 minutes, or until meat is no longer pink and vegetables are tender, stirring 2 or 3 times during cooking.

Blend cornstarch into reserved tomato juice. Add cornstarch mixture, tomatoes, curry, parsley, salt and pepper to meat mixture. Stir to break apart tomatoes. Microwave at High 7 to 12 minutes, or until meat is tender and flavors are blended.

Per Serving:
Calories:　　194
Sodium:　　282 mg.
Cholesterol:　118 mg.

BEEF BURGUNDY ▼

¼ cup water
¼ cup burgundy wine
1 tablespoon cornstarch
1 lb. boneless sirloin, cut into
    ¾-in. cubes
1 medium onion, chopped
8 oz. sliced fresh mushrooms
½ teaspoon salt, optional
¼ teaspoon thyme leaves
¼ teaspoon pepper

Serves 4

Blend water, wine and cornstarch in 3-qt. casserole. Stir in remaining ingredients; cover. Microwave at High 3 minutes. Reduce power to 50% (Medium). Microwave 20 to 30 minutes, or until meat is fork tender, stirring once or twice. Let stand, covered, 5 minutes.

Per Serving:
Calories: 198
Sodium: 322 mg.
Cholesterol: 77 mg.

SPAGHETTI SAUCE ▲

1 lb. extra lean ground beef
1 medium onion, chopped
1 can (6 oz.) tomato paste
1 can (16 oz.) whole tomatoes
2 tablespoons grated
    Parmesan cheese
½ cup water
2 teaspoons snipped fresh
    parsley
1 teaspoon oregano leaves
1 teaspoon basil leaves
½ teaspoon salt, optional
¼ teaspoon pepper
⅛ teaspoon ground nutmeg

Serves 4

In 2-qt. casserole combine crumbled ground beef and onion. Microwave at High 4 to 6 minutes, or until meat is no longer pink, stirring after half the time. Stir in remaining ingredients. Microwave at High 5 minutes. Reduce power to 50% (Medium). Microwave 15 to 20 minutes, or until sauce thickens and flavors blend, stirring 2 or 3 times.

Per Serving:
Calories: 248
Sodium: 550 mg.
Cholesterol: 85 mg.

BURGERS WITH MUSHROOM SAUCE

1 lb. extra lean ground beef
1 tablespoon instant minced
   onion
1 tablespoon dry vegetable
   flakes
1 teaspoon Worcestershire
   sauce
½ teaspoon salt, optional
¼ teaspoon pepper
⅛ teaspoon garlic powder
1 teaspoon prepared
   horseradish
8 oz. sliced fresh mushrooms
1 teaspoon soy sauce
¼ teaspoon dry mustard
¼ cup white wine
1 tablespoon cornstarch
¼ cup water

Serves 4

In medium mixing bowl combine ground beef, minced onion, vegetable flakes, Worcestershire sauce, salt, pepper, garlic powder and horseradish. Form into 4 patties. Place in 12 × 8-in. baking dish.

Microwave at High 5 to 9 minutes, or until meat is no longer pink, rearranging after half the cooking time. Remove patties and set aside, reserving meat juices.

Add remaining ingredients to meat juices. Microwave at High 6 to 9 minutes, or until sauce is thickened and mushrooms are tender, stirring 2 or 3 times. Return patties to dish. Microwave at High 1 to 2 minutes, or until just heated through.

NOTE: for low sodium diet substitute low-salt soy sauce.

Per Serving:
  Calories: 198
  Sodium: 425 mg.
  Cholesterol: 77 mg.

CHILI WITH ROUND STEAK

1½ lbs. round steak, cut into
    ¾-in. cubes
1 medium green pepper,
   chopped
1 medium onion, chopped
1 clove garlic, minced
2 to 3 teaspoons chili powder
1 teaspoon ground cumin
⅛ teaspoon pepper
2 cans (16 oz. each) whole
   tomatoes, undrained
1 can (15½ oz.) kidney beans,
   drained and rinsed

Serves 6

In 3-qt. casserole combine all ingredients; cover. Microwave at High 5 minutes. Remove cover. Stir to break apart tomatoes. Reduce power to 50% (Medium). Microwave, uncovered, 40 to 60 minutes, or until meat is fork tender, stirring 2 or 3 times. Let stand, covered, 10 minutes.

Per Serving:
  Calories: 254
  Sodium: 154 mg.
  Cholesterol: 77 mg.

BEEF STEW

1 lb. chuck stew meat
1 medium potato, cut into
   ½-in. chunks
1 medium onion, cut into
   eighths
3 medium stalks celery, sliced
3 medium carrots, sliced
½ teaspoon rosemary leaves
½ teaspoon salt, optional
¼ teaspoon pepper
½ teaspoon marjoram leaves
2 medium tomatoes, chopped
1 can (12 oz.) light beer
¼ cup water
1 tablespoon cornstarch

Serves 6

In 3-qt. casserole combine all ingredients except water and cornstarch. In 1-cup measure blend water and cornstarch; stir into casserole. Cover. Microwave at High 10 minutes. Reduce power to 50% (Medium). Microwave 45 to 60 minutes, or until meat is fork tender, stirring once or twice. Let stand, covered, 5 to 10 minutes.

Per Serving:
  Calories: 160
  Sodium: 244 mg.
  Cholesterol: 52 mg.

STUFFED PEPPERS ▶

1 lb. extra lean ground beef
1 medium onion, chopped
1 medium tomato, chopped
1 cup cooked rice
¼ teaspoon marjoram leaves
   Dash cayenne pepper
4 large green peppers, seeds
   and pulp removed
1 slice low fat cheese, cut
   into 8 thin strips

Serves 4

In medium mixing bowl combine crumbled ground beef, onion, tomato, rice and seasonings. Mix well. Fill green peppers with meat mixture.

Place a few wooden picks around bottom of peppers to hold up if needed.

Place on roasting rack. Cover with wax paper. Microwave at High 13 to 17 minutes, or until meat is no longer pink and peppers are tender, rearranging after half the cooking time. Cut each cheese strip into halves; top each pepper with four halves. Microwave 1 to 2 minutes, or until cheese melts.

Per Serving:
  Calories: 246
  Sodium: 137 mg.
  Cholesterol: 79 mg.

CABBAGE ROLLS ▲

8 medium cabbage leaves

Filling:

1 lb. extra lean ground beef
1 egg
¼ cup chopped onion
¼ cup chopped green pepper
1 teaspoon Worcestershire
   sauce
⅛ teaspoon garlic powder
1 teaspoon prepared hot
   mustard
¼ teaspoon salt, optional
⅛ teaspoon pepper
1 teaspoon prepared
   horseradish

Sauce:

1 cup tomato juice
¼ teaspoon basil leaves
½ teaspoon oregano leaves
2 to 3 drops hot red pepper
   sauce

Serves 4

Microwave whole cabbage at High 2 minutes, or until 8 outer leaves can be separated easily. Remove stem end of each leaf by cutting a 'V'. Arrange leaves in 12 × 8-in. baking dish. Cover with plastic wrap. Microwave at High 2 to 4 minutes, or until leaves are tender and pliable.

In medium bowl blend all filling ingredients. Place one-eighth of the meat mixture on base of each leaf. Fold in sides of leaf; roll up. Place seam side down in 12 × 8-in. baking dish

Combine sauce ingredients. Pour over rolls; cover. Microwave at High 7 to 12 minutes, or until centers of rolls are no longer pink, rearranging rolls after half the cooking time.

NOTE: for low sodium diet substitute low-salt tomato juice.

Per Serving:
Calories: 190
Sodium: 359 mg.
Cholesterol: 110 mg.

TACO DINNER SALAD

1 lb. extra lean ground beef
⅓ cup chopped green onion
¼ cup catsup
2 teaspoons chili powder
½ teaspoon ground cumin
½ teaspoon paprika
½ teaspoon salt, optional
¼ teaspoon pepper
6 cups shredded lettuce
2 large tomatoes, chopped

Serves 4

In 1-qt. casserole combine crumbled ground beef and onion. Microwave at High 4 to 8 minutes, or until beef is no longer pink, stirring once or twice. Drain well. Stir in catsup, chili powder, cumin, paprika, salt and pepper. Microwave at High 1½ to 3½ minutes, or until very hot, stirring once or twice.

Divide lettuce and tomatoes into 4 serving bowls. Add one-fourth ground beef mixture to each bowl; toss if desired.

NOTE: for low sodium diet substitute low-salt catsup.

Per Serving:
Calories: 195
Sodium: 504 mg.
Cholesterol: 77 mg.

PORK TENDERLOIN

1 teaspoon parsley flakes
⅛ teaspoon garlic powder
⅛ teaspoon pepper
2 lb. pork tenderloin roast

Serves 8

Cooking time: 12½ to 16½ minutes per lb.

Combine seasonings. Rub well over surface of roast. Place tenderloin on roasting rack in 12 × 8-in. baking dish. Shield ends of roast with aluminum foil. Estimate total cooking time; divide in half. Microwave at High 3 minutes. Reduce power to 50% (Medium). Microwave remaining part of first half of time. Remove foil. Turn roast over. Spread one of the fruit glazes, page 24, over roast, if desired. Microwave at 50% (Medium) the remaining time, or until the internal temperature reaches 165°. Tent loosely with foil. Let stand 5 to 10 minutes, or until temperature is 170°.

Per Serving:
Calories: 256
Sodium: 69 mg.
Cholesterol: 75 mg.

PINEAPPLE GLAZE ▼

1 can (8 oz.) crushed
    pineapple, drained
1 teaspoon prepared mustard
1 teaspoon ground ginger
1 teaspoon brown sugar

Makes 1 cup
Serving size: 2 tablespoons

Combine ingredients in small bowl
or 2-cup measure. Microwave
at High 1 to 2 minutes, or until
heated. Spread over pork tenderloin
roast as directed.

Per Serving:
  Calories: 17
  Sodium: 0
  Cholesterol: 0

APPLE GLAZE

½ cup unsweetened
    applesauce
¼ teaspoon nutmeg
½ teaspoon cinnamon

Makes ½ cup
Serving size: 1 tablespoon

Mix applesauce, nutmeg and
cinnamon. Spread on pork
tenderloin roast as directed.

Per Serving:
  Calories: 5
  Sodium: 0
  Cholesterol: 0

BAVARIAN PORK CHOPS ▶

1 can (16 oz.) sauerkraut,
   drained
1 teaspoon vinegar
1 teaspoon brown sugar
¼ teaspoon cinnamon
   Dash salt, optional
   Dash pepper
¼ teaspoon caraway seed
1 medium apple, diced
4 lean pork chops, ½ in. thick
2 teaspoons Worcestershire
   sauce

Serves 4

In 8×8-in. baking dish, combine
sauerkraut, vinegar, brown sugar,
cinnamon, salt, pepper, caraway
and apple. Top with pork chops.
Brush each chop with Worcestershire sauce. Cover with
waxed paper.

Microwave at High 5 minutes.
Rearrange chops; reduce power to
50% (Medium). Microwave 7 to 15
minutes, or until meat near bone
is no longer pink.

Per Serving:
Calories:	274
Sodium:	268 mg.
Cholesterol:	76 mg.

BASIC PORK CHOPS

1½ teaspoons bouquet sauce
 2 teaspoons water
 4 lean pork chops, ½ in.
    thick

Serves 4

Cooking Time: 16½ to 18½
                 minutes per lb.

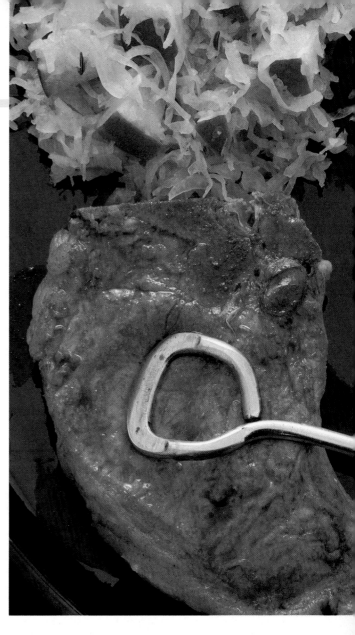

In small dish, combine bouquet
sauce and water. Place pork chops
on roasting rack; brush with half
of bouquet sauce mixture. Cover
with wax paper. Estimate total
cooking time. Microwave at 50%
(Medium) for half the total
cooking time. Turn over and
rearrange chops. Brush with
remaining bouquet mixture.
Microwave at 50% (Medium) for
remaining time, or until meat is
no longer pink.

Per Serving:
Calories:	234
Sodium:	173 mg.
Cholesterol:	76 mg.

PORK CHOP BAKE ▼

4 lean pork chops, ½ in. thick
4 thin onion slices
4 green pepper rings
1 medium tomato, sliced
2 tablespoons Parmesan cheese
  Paprika

Serves 4

Preheat 10-in. browning dish at High 5 minutes. Place pork chops on dish. When sizzling stops, turn chops over and top with onion and green pepper. Reduce power to 50% (Medium). Microwave 7 to 10 minutes, or until meat is no longer pink; rearrange chops after half the time. Top each chop with tomato slice and Parmesan cheese during last 2 minutes. Sprinkle with paprika.

Per Serving:
Calories: 262
Sodium: 57 mg.
Cholesterol: 84 mg.

PORK STEW ▶

1 cup hot water
1 teaspoon instant chicken
   bouillon granules
¼ teaspoon bouquet sauce
2 tablespoons all-purpose
   flour
1 lb. lean boneless pork, cut
   into 1-in. cubes
1 large onion, thinly sliced
1 cup thinly sliced celery
1 can (16 oz.) whole
   tomatoes
8 oz. green beans, cut into
   1-in. lengths
2 medium yellow squash,
   thinly sliced
½ teaspoon thyme leaves
¼ teaspoon salt, optional
   Dash pepper
1½ cups shredded lettuce

Serves 6

In 2-cup measure, blend hot water, bouillon, bouquet sauce and flour. Set aside.

Place remaining ingredients except lettuce in 3-qt. casserole. Stir in flour and water mixture. Cover. Microwave at High 10 minutes. Stir. Re-cover.

Reduce power to 50% (Medium). Microwave 35 to 40 minutes, or until meat and vegetables are tender. Stir in lettuce. Let stand, covered, 5 to 10 minutes.

NOTE: for low sodium diet substitute low-salt bouillon and bouquet sauce.

Per Serving:
  Calories: 240
  Sodium: 304 mg.
  Cholesterol: 49 mg.

◄ MUSHROOM VEAL

    1 lb. boneless veal, pounded
        to ¼-in. thickness, cut into
        serving pieces
    8 oz. sliced fresh mushrooms
    ⅓ cup water
    2 tablespoons apple juice
    2 teaspoons all-purpose flour
    1½ teaspoons freeze-dried
        chives
    2 teaspoons lemon juice
    ½ teaspoon instant beef
        bouillon granules
    ½ teaspoon onion powder
    ⅛ teaspoon salt, optional
    ⅛ teaspoon bouquet sauce

                        Serves 4

Arrange veal in 12 × 8-in. baking
dish. Top with sliced mushrooms.
Cover with wax paper. Microwave
at 50% (Medium) 7 to 10 minutes,
or until veal is tender and no
longer pink; rearrange veal once,
leaving mushrooms on top. Set
veal aside.

In small bowl blend remaining
ingredients. Increase power to
High. Microwave 1½ to 4 minutes,
or until thickened, stirring with
wire whip once or twice. Pour
sauce over the veal; cover with
wax paper.

Reduce power to 50% (Medium).
Microwave 1½ to 3½ minutes, or
until heated through.

    Per Serving:
      Calories: 180
      Sodium: 262 mg.
      Cholesterol: 86 mg.

VEAL MOZZARELLA

    1 can (8 oz.) tomato paste
    ¾ teaspoon Italian seasoning
    ⅛ teaspoon garlic powder
    ¼ teaspoon salt, optional
    ¼ teaspoon sugar
    ⅛ teaspoon pepper
    1 lb. boneless veal, pounded
        to ¼-in. thickness, cut into
        serving pieces
    ¾ cup shredded mozzarella
        cheese
    1 tablespoon parsley flakes

                        Serves 4

Combine all ingredients except
veal, cheese and parsley in small
bowl. Microwave at High 2
minutes. Reduce power to 50%
(Medium). Microwave 6 minutes.
Set aside.

Place veal in 12 × 8-in. baking dish.
Cover with wax paper. Microwave
at 50% (Medium) 6 to 9 minutes,
or until veal is no longer pink,
rearranging once. Drain. Cover
with sauce. Sprinkle mozzarella
cheese and parsley on top; cover
with wax paper.

Microwave at 50% (Medium) 3 to
7 minutes, or until sauce is hot and
cheese melts, rotating dish once.

    Per Serving:
      Calories: 280
      Sodium: 327 mg.
      Cholesterol: 100 mg.

MARINATED LAMB KABOBS

1 can (8 oz.) pineapple chunks
   in own juice, drained, juice
   reserved
2 tablespoons orange juice
2 teaspoons soy sauce
½ teaspoon ground coriander
⅛ teaspoon curry powder
¼ teaspoon dry mint leaves
1 lb. boneless lamb, cut into
   24 pieces
8 firm cherry tomatoes
½ medium green pepper, cut
   into eighths
4 wooden skewers, 12-in. long

Serves 4

In small bowl combine ⅓ cup reserved pineapple juice, orange juice, soy sauce, coriander, curry and mint leaves. Stir in meat; cover. Marinate overnight in refrigerator. Remove meat; discard marinade.

Alternate lamb, tomatoes, green peppers and pineapple chunks on skewers.

Arrange skewers on roasting rack. Microwave at 50% (Medium) 8 to 11 minutes, or until lamb is desired doneness.

NOTE: for low sodium diet substitute low-salt soy sauce.

Per Serving:
  Calories: 205
  Sodium: 234 mg.
  Cholesterol: 85 mg.

MARINATED LAMB CHOPS

¼ cup dry sherry
½ cup cider vinegar
2 green onions, finely
   chopped
1 clove garlic, minced
2 tablespoons lemon juice
2 teaspoons lemon pepper
   seasoning
1 teaspoon Worcestershire
   sauce
1 teaspoon crushed rosemary
   leaves
¼ teaspoon grated lemon peel
½ teaspoon bouquet sauce,
   optional
4 lamb loin chops, 1½-in.
   thick

Serves 4

Combine all ingredients except lamb chops in small bowl. Place chops in plastic bag, pour in marinade and seal. Marinate in refrigerator overnight.

Arrange lamb chops on roasting rack. Discard marinade. Microwave at High 5 minutes. Turn chops over. Reduce power to 50% (Medium). Microwave 7 to 9 minutes, or until lamb chops have reached desired doneness.

Per Serving:
  Calories: 193
  Sodium: 144 mg.
  Cholesterol: 85 mg.

MIDDLE EASTERN ▲ LAMB MEATBALLS

Meatballs:
- 1 lb. lean ground lamb
- 1 small onion, finely chopped
- ½ teaspoon dry mint leaves
- ½ teaspoon oregano leaves
- ½ teaspoon salt, optional
- ¼ teaspoon ground cinnamon
- ¼ teaspoon ground cumin
- ⅛ teaspoon cayenne

Sauce:
- 3 tomatoes, peeled and coarsely chopped
- 1 small onion, chopped
- ½ cup chopped green pepper
- 2 teaspoons olive oil
- 2 teaspoons parsley flakes
- 1 teaspoon salt, optional

Serves 4

In medium bowl blend meatball ingredients. Shape into 12 meatballs. Place on roasting rack; cover with wax paper. Microwave at High 3 minutes. Rearrange meatballs. Microwave 1½ to 2½ minutes longer, or until meat is no longer pink. Set aside.

In 12 × 8-in. baking dish combine sauce ingredients; cover. Microwave at High 4 to 5 minutes, or until green pepper is tender. Add meatballs; cover. Microwave at High 1 to 2 minutes to reheat.

Per Serving:
Calories: 219
Sodium: 828 mg.
Cholesterol: 85 mg.

POULTRY

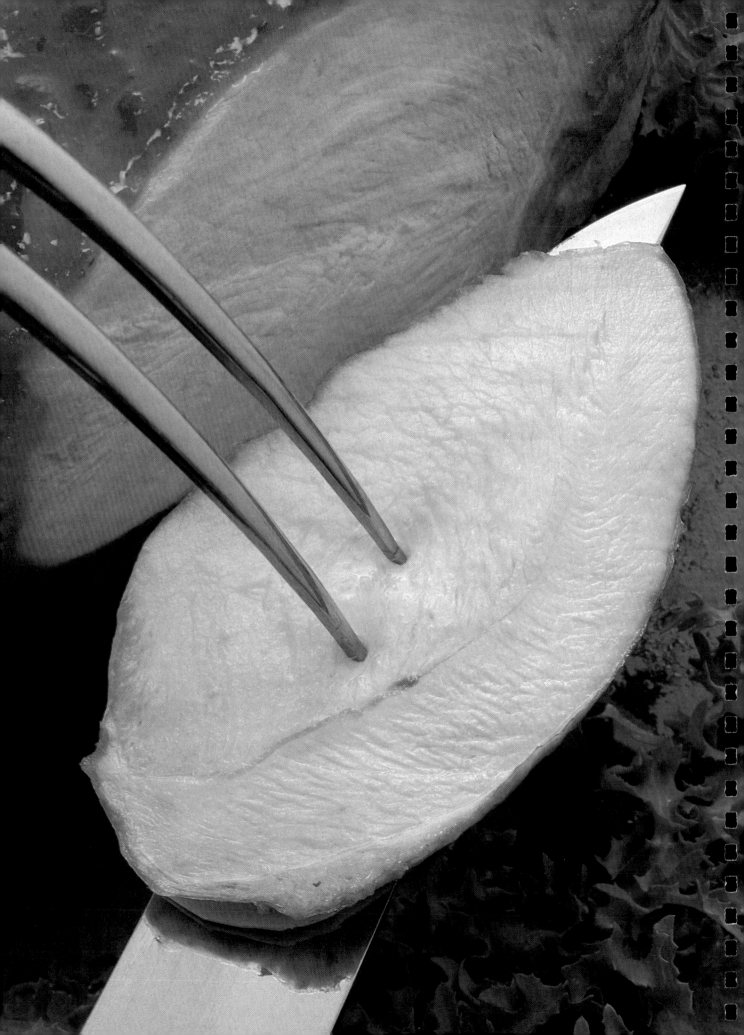

◄ GLAZED TURKEY BREAST

5 to 6-lb. turkey breast
¼ cup low sugar tart cherry
   preserves
¼ cup low sugar imitation
   apple jelly
¼ teaspoon poultry seasoning
¼ teaspoon dry mustard

Serves 10

Cooking time: 11 to 15
              minutes per lb.

Place turkey breast-side down
in baking dish. Estimate total
cooking time; divide in half.
Microwave at High 5 minutes.
Reduce power to 50% (Medium).
Microwave remainder of first half
of time. Turn. Blend preserves,
jelly, poultry seasoning and dry
mustard. Glaze turkey with half
of jelly mixture. Microwave for
second half of time, or until
internal temperature is 170°; glaze
with remaining jelly during last
10 minutes.

Per Serving:
Calories: 188
Sodium: 75 mg.
Cholesterol: 71 mg.

VEGETABLE BRAISED TURKEY

1 large tomato, coarsely
  chopped
1 large onion, sliced and
  separated into rings
1 stalk celery, chopped
1 medium green pepper, cut
  into thin strips
2 turkey thighs (2½ to 3 lbs.)
  boned and skin removed
¼ cup hot water
½ teaspoon instant chicken
  bouillon granules
¼ teaspoon pepper
¼ teaspoon salt, optional
½ teaspoon red wine vinegar
⅛ teaspoon ground sage

Serves 4

Combine tomato, onion, celery
and green pepper in 8 × 8-in.
baking dish. Place turkey thighs
on top of vegetables with meatiest
portions to outside of dish.

In 1-cup measure combine remaining ingredients. Pour over turkey
and vegetables. Cover with plastic
wrap. Microwave at High 3 minutes. Rotate and rearrange pieces.
Reduce power to 50% (Medium).
Microwave 30 to 35 minutes, or
until meat is no longer pink,
rotating and rearranging meat
twice during cooking.

Per Serving:
Calories: 184
Sodium: 147 mg.
Cholesterol: 60 mg.

SWEET & SOUR TURKEY

1 pkg. (6 oz.) frozen pea
   pods
2 tablespoons water
1 medium onion, thinly
   sliced
¼ cup chopped green pepper
1 large stalk celery, sliced
   diagonally
2 cups cooked, cubed turkey
1 can (15½ oz.) pineapple
   chunks, packed in own juice,
   juice reserved
4 teaspoons cornstarch
1 teaspoon instant chicken
   bouillon granules
⅛ teaspoon ground ginger
¼ teaspoon salt, optional
   Dash cayenne
1 teaspoon brown sugar
1½ tablespoons soy sauce
1 tablespoon vinegar

Serves 4

Place pea pods and water in 2-qt. casserole; cover. Microwave at High 2 to 3 minutes, or until defrosted. Break apart and drain. Stir in onion, green pepper, celery, turkey, and pineapple chunks. Set aside.

In 4-cup measure combine corn-starch, bouillon, ginger, salt, cayenne and brown sugar. Stir in soy sauce, vinegar and pineapple juice. Microwave at High 2 to 3½ minutes, or until sauce is clear and thickened, stirring every minute.

Fold sauce into turkey mixture; cover. Microwave at High 4 to 6 minutes, or until heated through.

NOTE: for low sodium diet substitute low-salt soy sauce and bouillon.

Per Serving:
Calories: 188
Sodium: 534 mg.
Cholesterol: 35 mg.

SWEET & SOUR SAUCE

½ cup unsweetened pineapple
   juice
5 tablespoons catsup
2 teaspoons white wine
   vinegar
½ cup water
1 teaspoon instant minced
   onion
3 drops hot red pepper sauce

Serves 11
Serving size: 2 tablespoons

Combine all ingredients in 2-cup measure. Microwave at High 3 to 6 minutes, or until sauce is bubbly and onion is tender. Serve with beef, pork, chicken or vegetables.

NOTE: for low sodium diet substitute low-salt catsup.

Per Serving:
Calories: 11
Sodium: 82 mg.
Cholesterol: 0

TURKEY CHOW MEIN

2 turkey thighs (1¼ lbs. each)
   boned, cut into ½-in. cubes
2 tablespoons cornstarch
¼ cup water
2 teaspoons instant chicken
   bouillon granules
2 tablespoons soy sauce
1 cup thinly sliced celery
⅔ cup chopped onion
1 can (16 oz.) chow mein
   vegetables, drained
8 oz. fresh sliced mushrooms
⅛ teaspoon ground ginger
⅛ teaspoon pepper
½ cup chow mein noodles

Serves 6

Place turkey pieces in 2-qt.
casserole; cover. Microwave at
High 5 to 6 minutes, or until meat
is no longer pink, stirring after
half the time. Drain.

Blend cornstarch and water. Add
to casserole. Stir in all remaining
ingredients except noodles; cover.
Microwave at High 10 to 12
minutes, or until sauce thickens
and vegetables are hot, stirring 2
or 3 times. Top casserole with
chow mein noodles.

NOTE: for low sodium diet use
low-salt soy sauce and bouillon.

Per Serving:
   Calories: 167
   Sodium: 455 mg.
   Cholesterol: 43 mg.

TURKEY STUFFED TOMATOES

4 large tomatoes
1 pkg. (10 oz.) frozen
   artichoke hearts
2 cups cooked, cubed turkey
1 tablespoon grated Parmesan
   cheese
¼ teaspoon onion powder
¼ teaspoon basil leaves
¼ teaspoon freeze-dried chives
¼ teaspoon salt, optional
⅛ teaspoon pepper
   Paprika

Serves 4

Cut a thin slice from stem end of
each tomato. Scoop out pulp. Pulp
can be frozen for future use in
various sauces.

Place artichoke package in oven.
Microwave at High 1½ to 4
minutes, or until package flexes
easily. Drain. Chop artichokes into
small pieces.

In medium mixing bowl combine
artichokes, turkey, Parmesan,
onion powder, basil, chives, salt
and pepper. Spoon into tomato
shells. Sprinkle with paprika.
Place each tomato in custard cup
or small bowl. Microwave at High
5 to 8 minutes, or until heated.

Per Serving:
   Calories: 135
   Sodium: 181 mg.
   Cholesterol: 39 mg.

CHICKEN BREAST ▲ CACCIATORE

1 can (16 oz.) whole tomatoes, cut up
½ medium green pepper, cut into thin strips
1 medium onion, sliced and separated into rings
¼ cup dry white wine
1 teaspoon Italian seasoning
¼ teaspoon salt, optional
2 whole bone-in chicken breasts, halved, skin removed
1 pkg. (7 oz.) vermicelli, cooked
2 tablespoons grated Romano cheese

Serves 4

In 2-qt. casserole combine tomatoes, green pepper, onion, wine and seasonings; cover. Microwave at High 5 to 7 minutes, or until vegetables are tender, stirring once.

Arrange chicken in 12 × 8-in. baking dish with meatiest portions to outside of dish. Pour sauce and vegetables over chicken. Cover with wax paper. Microwave at High 14 to 18 minutes, or until chicken is tender and no longer pink; rearrange and spoon sauce over chicken twice during cooking time.

Serve chicken over vermicelli that has been tossed with grated Romano cheese.

Per Serving:
Calories: 360
Sodium: 356 mg.
Cholesterol: 71 mg.

LEMON SEASONED CHICKEN BREASTS

1 tablespoon water
½ teaspoon bouquet sauce
1 tablespoon lemon juice
1 teaspoon lemon pepper
    seasoning
½ teaspoon salt, optional
⅛ teaspoon poultry seasoning
    Dash garlic powder
2 whole bone-in chicken
    breasts, halved, skin removed
1 to 2 teaspoons parsley flakes

Serves 4

In small dish combine all ingredients except chicken and parsley. Arrange chicken breasts bone-side up on microwave roasting rack, with meatiest portions to outside of dish. Brush with half of seasoned mixture. Microwave at High 5 minutes.

Turn pieces over and brush with remaining mixture. Microwave 10 to 15 minutes, or until meat near bone is no longer pink, rotating once during cooking. If desired, sprinkle with parsley flakes before serving.

Per Serving:
  Calories: 165
  Sodium: 132 mg.
  Cholesterol: 63 mg.

MEXICAN CHICKEN

1 medium green pepper,
    thinly sliced
1 small onion, sliced and
    separated into rings
8 oz. fresh sliced mushrooms
1 can (4 oz.) chopped green
    chilies, drained
2 whole bone-in chicken
    breasts, halved, skin removed
¼ teaspoon chili powder
¼ teaspoon oregano leaves
    Dash cayenne pepper
⅛ teaspoon garlic powder
1 can (15 oz.) tomato sauce

Serves 4

In 12 × 8-in. baking dish combine green pepper, onion, mushrooms and chilies. Cover with wax paper. Microwave at High 4 to 5 minutes, or until pepper is tender-crisp, stirring once. Drain.

Arrange chicken breasts over vegetables, bone-side up, with meatiest portions to outside of dish. Combine spices and tomato sauce. Pour half of tomato sauce mixture over chicken. Cover with wax paper. Microwave at High 10 to 16 minutes, or until chicken is opaque and tender. Turn over, rearrange and cover chicken with remaining sauce after half the time.

Per Serving:
  Calories: 260
  Sodium: 229 mg.
  Cholesterol: 63 mg.

CHICKEN & BROCCOLI ▲

3 tablespoons water
1 tablespoon teriyaki sauce
1 tablespoon cornstarch
1 teaspoon fructose
1 teaspoon instant chicken
   bouillon granules
⅛ teaspoon garlic powder
1 tablespoon vegetable oil
4 green onions
2 whole boneless chicken
   breasts, skin removed, cut
   into strips
3 to 3½ cups fresh broccoli
   flowerets
4 oz. fresh sliced mushrooms

Serves 4

In small bowl combine water,
teriyaki sauce, cornstarch,
fructose, chicken bouillon and
garlic powder. Set aside.

Preheat 10-in. browning dish
at High 5 minutes. Pour in oil.
Add onions, chicken strips and
broccoli. Stir until sizzling stops;
cover. Microwave at High 3½ to
4½ minutes, or until chicken is
no longer pink and broccoli is
tender-crisp.

Add mushrooms and teriyaki
sauce mixture, stirring to coat
chicken. Microwave 2 to 3
minutes, or until sauce thickens
slightly, mushrooms are tender,
and mixture is heated through,
stirring 2 or 3 times.

NOTE: For low sodium diet substitute low-salt teriyaki sauce and
bouillon.

Per Serving:	
Calories:	249
Sodium:	676 mg.
Cholesterol:	63 mg.

CHICKEN BREASTS IN MUSHROOM SAUCE ▼

8 oz. fresh sliced mushrooms
¼ cup chopped green onions
1 tablespoon margarine or
   butter
2 tablespoons all-purpose flour
2 tablespoons dry sherry
¼ cup water
½ cup plain low fat yogurt
½ teaspoon salt, optional
⅛ teaspoon white pepper
1 teaspoon instant chicken
   bouillon granules
2 whole boneless chicken
   breasts, halved, skin removed

Serves 4

Combine mushrooms and onions in 1-qt. casserole. Cover. Microwave at High 3 to 4½ minutes, or until mushrooms are tender. Drain well. Place margarine in 4-cup measure.

Microwave at High 30 seconds to 1½ minutes, or until melted. Blend in flour. Add sherry, water, yogurt, salt, pepper and bouillon. Stir in mushrooms and onions.

Arrange chicken in 8 × 8-in. baking dish. Pour sauce over chicken. Cover with wax paper. Reduce power to 50% (Medium). Microwave 14 to 20 minutes, or until sauce thickens and chicken is tender and no longer pink. Turn and rearrange breasts and stir sauce every 5 minutes during cooking. Serve sauce over chicken.

NOTE: for low sodium diet substitute low-salt bouillon.

Per Serving:
  Calories: 249
  Sodium: 527 mg.
  Cholesterol: 65 mg.

BARBECUE CHICKEN DRUMSTICKS ▼

¼ cup chopped onion
2 tablespoons chopped celery
½ teaspoon sugar
½ teaspoon dry mustard
1 teaspoon Worcestershire
   sauce
1 tablespoon cider vinegar
¾ cup catsup
⅛ teaspoon pepper
2 tablespoons water
2 to 3 drops hot red pepper
   sauce
⅛ teaspoon chili powder
8 chicken drumsticks, skin
   removed

Serves 4

Combine all ingredients except drumsticks in 4-cup measure. Cover with wax paper. Microwave at High 3 minutes, or until hot, stirring once. Reduce power to 50% (Medium). Microwave 13 to 19 minutes, or until vegetables are tender and flavors are blended, stirring every 2 or 3 minutes.

Arrange drumsticks on roasting rack with meatiest portions to outside. Brush with one-third of sauce. Cover with wax paper. Increase power to High. Microwave 7 minutes. Turn over and rearrange legs; brush with one-third of sauce; cover. Microwave at High 4 minutes. Brush with remaining sauce; cover. Microwave 1 to 4 minutes, or until meat is no longer pink and sauce is hot.

NOTE: for low sodium diet substitute low-salt catsup.

Per Serving:
Calories:	210
Sodium:	518 mg.
Cholesterol:	78 mg.

SOY GARLIC GLAZE

2 teaspoons soy sauce
1 tablespoon white wine
  Water
1 teaspoon cornstarch
¼ teaspoon dry mustard
⅛ teaspoon garlic powder

Glazes 2 Cornish hens

In 1-cup measure combine soy sauce and wine. Add water to equal ½ cup. Blend in cornstarch, dry mustard and garlic powder. Microwave at High 1 to 3 minutes, or until thickened; stir once. Baste 2 hens with half of glaze. Microwave as directed below, basting when turning. Serve with any remaining glaze.

Per Serving:
Calories: 11
Sodium: 345 mg.
Cholesterol: 0

CORNISH GAME HENS

2 Cornish game hens (1 to
  1½ lbs. each)
1½ teaspoons bouquet sauce,
  optional
2 teaspoons water, optional
¼ teaspoon poultry seasoning
  Dash pepper

Serves 2

Cooking time: 7 to 9 minutes
per lb.

Place hens on roasting rack breast-side down. Mix bouquet sauce with water and seasonings, and brush half of sauce over hens, or use Soy Garlic Glaze, above. Estimate total cooking time. Microwave at High for half the time. Turn hens breast-side up; rearrange. Baste with remaining bouquet sauce or glaze. Microwave at High for remaining time, or until legs move freely and juices run clear.

Per Serving:
Calories: 234
Sodium: 364 mg.
Cholesterol: 181 mg.

VEGETABLE RICE STUFFING

½ cup thinly sliced carrots
1 cup thinly sliced celery
¼ cup chopped onion
½ cup cooked rice
¼ teaspoon bouquet garni
  seasoning
  Dash pepper

Stuffs 2 Cornish hens

Combine all ingredients in 1-qt. casserole; cover. Microwave at High 1 to 3 minutes, or until celery is tender-crisp. Stuff 2 hens loosely and microwave as directed.

Per Serving:
Calories: 73
Sodium: 58 mg.
Cholesterol: 0

FISH & SEAFOOD

SOLE FLORENTINE ▲

  2 pkgs. (10 oz. each) frozen
      chopped spinach
  1 tablespoon dry minced
      onion
  ½ teaspoon grated lemon peel
  ½ teaspoon salt, optional
  ¼ teaspoon pepper
  ½ teaspoon dry mustard
      Dash ground nutmeg
  2 tablespoons grated
      Parmesan cheese
  1 teaspoon parsley flakes
  ½ teaspoon paprika
  1 lb. sole fillets

Serves 4

Place spinach packages in oven.
Microwave at High 6 to 6½
minutes, or until package flexes
easily. Rearrange once. Drain

spinach well. Place in 8 × 8-in.
baking dish. Stir in onion, lemon
peel, salt, pepper, dry mustard
and nutmeg. Spread spinach
mixture evenly over bottom of
baking dish.

Combine Parmesan, parsley and
paprika. Set aside. Place fish on
top of spinach mixture. Cover
with wax paper. Microwave at
High 4 minutes; rearrange and
sprinkle with Parmesan mixture.
Cover. Microwave at High 2 to 6
minutes, or until fish flakes easily
with fork.

Per Serving:
Calories: 155
Sodium: 326 mg.
Cholesterol: 70 mg.

GRILLED TUNA STEAKS

1 lb. fresh tuna, cut into
   4 steaks
   Dash white pepper

Serves 4

Remove skin from tuna. Sprinkle with pepper. Preheat 10-in. browning dish at High 5 minutes. Add steaks. Microwave at High 1 minute. Turn and rearrange. Microwave at High 1 to 3 minutes, or until fish flakes easily and is no longer pink.

Per Serving:
Calories: 165
Sodium: 42 mg.
Cholesterol: 71 mg.

RED SNAPPER

⅛ to ¼ teaspoon tarragon
   leaves
½ teaspoon parsley flakes
⅛ teaspoon pepper
½ teaspoon onion powder
1 lb. red snapper fillets
6 to 8 slices lemon

Serves 4

Combine tarragon, parsley, pepper and onion powder. Arrange fish in 8 × 8-in. baking dish. Sprinkle with seasoning mixture. Cover with wax paper. Microwave at High 3 minutes; rearrange pieces and top each with a slice of lemon; cover. Microwave at High 2½ to 4½ minutes, or until fish flakes easily with fork.

Per Serving:
Calories: 113
Sodium: 40 mg.
Cholesterol: 63 mg.

STEAMED TROUT WITH WINE & LEMON

1 lb. trout fillets
4 slices lemon
¼ cup white wine
¼ cup chopped onion
1 teaspoon grated lemon peel
⅛ teaspoon white pepper
⅛ teaspoon ground coriander
1 teaspoon parsley flakes

Serves 4

Arrange fish in 12 × 8-in. baking dish. Top with lemon slices. In 1-cup measure combine wine, onion, lemon peel, pepper, coriander and parsley. Pour over fish. Cover with wax paper. Microwave at High 4 to 7 minutes, or until fish flakes easily, rearranging after half the cooking time.

Per Serving:
Calories: 128
Sodium: 50 mg.
Cholesterol: 62 mg.

PARMESAN SCALLOPS

3 green onions, chopped
8 oz. sliced fresh mushrooms
1 clove garlic, minced
¼ cup white wine
2 tablespoons lemon juice
1 small bay leaf
1 teaspoon dry mustard
½ teaspoon instant chicken
    bouillon granules
¼ teaspoon thyme leaves
1 tablespoon all-purpose flour
1 lb. scallops, rinsed and
    drained

Topping:
1 tablespoon dry bread
    crumbs
1½ teaspoons grated Parmesan
    cheese
½ teaspoon paprika
½ teaspoon parsley flakes

Serves 4

In 2-qt. casserole combine all ingredients except scallops and topping ingredients. Stir in scallops; cover. Microwave at 50% (Medium) 7 to 10 minutes, or until scallops are opaque and flaky, stirring every 2 minutes. Remove bay leaf.

Divide scallops and cooking liquid into 4 individual dishes. Combine bread crumbs, Parmesan, paprika and parsley to make topping. Sprinkle scallops with bread mixture. Microwave at 50% (Medium) 1 to 2 minutes, or until heated.

NOTE: for low sodium diet substitute low-salt bouillon.

Per Serving:
Calories: 133
Sodium: 416 mg.
Cholesterol: 47 mg.

EASY SHRIMP CREOLE

1 can (16 oz.) whole tomatoes
1 medium onion, chopped
1 green pepper, chopped
½ teaspoon salt, optional
¼ teaspoon pepper
¼ teaspoon basil leaves
½ teaspoon chili powder
    Dash cayenne
1 medium bay leaf
1 lb. fresh shrimp, shelled
    and deveined

Serves

Combine all ingredients except shrimp in 1½-qt. casserole, breaking up tomatoes with spoon cover. Microwave at High 8 to 12 minutes, or until green pepper is tender and sauce is bubbly, stirring once. Stir in shrimp; cover. Microwave at High 3 to 5 minutes, or until shrimp are just opaque, stirring once or twice. D not overcook. Let stand 3 to 5 minutes. Remove bay leaf.

Per Serving:
Calories: 141
Sodium: 345 mg.
Cholesterol: 170 mg.

SEAFOOD STEW

1 medium onion, chopped
1 clove garlic, minced
1 stalk celery, chopped
¼ cup water
½ teaspoon instant chicken
    bouillon granules
1 cup white wine
1 cup tomato juice
1 lb. fish fillets, cut into 1-in.
    cubes
2 tomatoes, cut into small
    wedges
2 teaspoons parsley flakes
⅛ teaspoon ground turmeric
⅛ teaspoon fennel seed
½ teaspoon thyme leaves
¼ teaspoon rubbed sage leaves
¼ teaspoon pepper
1 bay leaf
1 lb. fresh shrimp, shelled and
    deveined
6 oz. cooked crab legs, cut
    into 2-in. sections

Serves 6

In 5-qt. casserole combine onion, garlic, celery, water and bouillon; cover. Microwave at High 4 to 6 minutes, or until onion is tender, stirring after half the time. Stir in remaining ingredients except shrimp and crab; cover.

Microwave at High 10 to 12 minutes, or until fish is opaque, stirring twice. Mix in shrimp and crab meat; cover.

Microwave at High 4 to 5 minutes, or until shrimp are white, stirring after half the time. Let stand 2 to 3 minutes. Remove the bay leaf before serving.

Per Serving:
Calories: 221
Sodium: 374 mg.
Cholesterol: 115 mg.

SEAFOOD KABOBS

4 wooden skewers, 12-in. long
1 large green pepper, cut into
    1-in. chunks
1 lb. scallops (about 22 to 25),
    halved
½ medium onion, cut into
    wedges
4 cherry tomatoes
2 tablespoons soy sauce
1 teaspoon lemon juice
¼ teaspoon paprika
¼ teaspoon garlic powder

Serves 4

On each of 4 skewers alternate green pepper chunk, scallop half and onion wedge, with a cherry tomato in the center of skewer. In small bowl combine soy sauce, lemon juice, paprika and garlic powder. Place skewers on roasting rack; brush with half of sauce. Cover with wax paper. Microwave at 50% (Medium) 12 to 15 minutes, or until scallops are opaque and pepper is tender; rearrange and brush with sauce after half the cooking time.

NOTE: For low sodium diet substitute low-salt soy sauce.

Per Serving:
Calories: 104
Sodium: 807 mg.
Cholesterol: 45 mg.

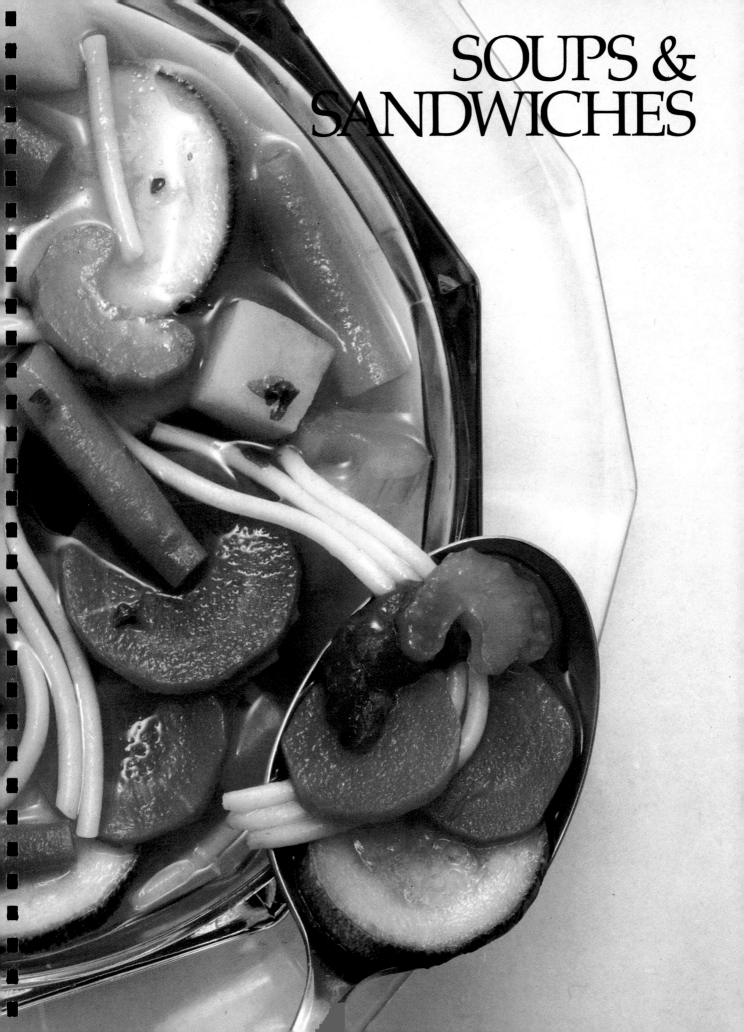

SOUPS &
SANDWICHES

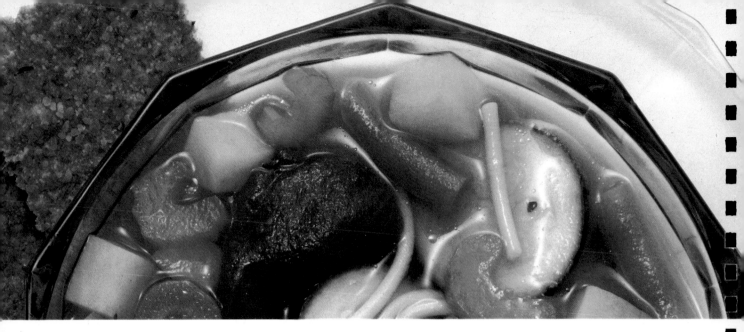

MINESTRONE ▲

½ cup thinly sliced celery
½ cup thinly sliced carrot
2 cloves garlic, minced
¾ cup (1 large) potato, cut into
    ½-in. cubes
1 can (16 oz.) tomatoes,
    undrained
1 cup thinly sliced zucchini
½ lb. green beans, cut into
    1-in. pieces
½ cup broken spaghetti
3 cups hot water
2 teaspoons instant beef
    bouillon granules
2 teaspoons basil leaves
1 tablespoon parsley flakes
1 bay leaf

Serves 6

In 3-qt. casserole combine all
ingredients.. Cover. Microwave at
High 25 to 35 minutes, or until
vegetables are tender, stirring
once or twice. Remove bay leaf
before serving.

NOTE: for low sodium diet
substitute low-salt bouillon.

Per Serving:
Calories: 35
Sodium: 315 mg.
Cholesterol: 0

PUMPKIN SOUP

5 green onions, chopped
2 tablespoons margarine or
    butter
1 can (16 oz.) pumpkin
¼ teaspoon ground ginger
⅛ teaspoon ground turmeric
⅛ teaspoon ground nutmeg
1 cup evaporated skim milk
1 cup skim milk
2 cups hot water
1 teaspoon instant chicken
    bouillon granules
1 tablespoon sugar

Serves 4

Place onion and margarine in 3-qt.
casserole. Microwave at High 2½
to 3 minutes, or until onion is
tender, stirring once. Blend in
remaining ingredients. Microwave
at High 6 to 7 minutes, or until
heated, stirring every 2 minutes.

Per Serving:
Calories: 181
Sodium: 403 mg.
Cholesterol: 0

SPICY TOMATO SOUP ▼

2½ cups tomato juice or
    vegetable cocktail
  2 teaspoons instant beef
    bouillon granules
  1 teaspoon Worcestershire
    sauce
    Dash cayenne
  ½ teaspoon basil leaves
  ¼ teaspoon thyme leaves
  1 teaspoon parsley flakes
  ½ teaspoon sugar
  4 lemon slices, optional
  4 celery stalks, optional

Serves 4

Combine all ingredients in 1-qt. casserole; cover. Microwave at High 1½ to 4 minutes, or until heated. Pour into 4 serving bowls. Garnish each with a lemon slice and celery stalk.

NOTE: for low sodium diet substitute low-salt bouillon and tomato juice or vegetable cocktail.

Per Serving:
  Calories: 25
  Sodium: 700 mg.
  Cholesterol: 0

and return to casserole. Add 2 cups hot water and noodles. Cover. Microwave at High 8 to 10 minutes, or until water boils. Microwave at High 7 to 10 minutes, or until noodles are tender.

Per Serving:
Calories: 111
Sodium: 274 mg.
Cholesterol: 42 mg.

CABBAGE SOUP

  2 slices bacon, chopped
  6 cups chopped cabbage
  1 medium onion, sliced and
       separated into rings
 ¼ teaspoon dill weed
 ¼ teaspoon caraway seed
 ¼ teaspoon celery seed
 ⅛ teaspoon pepper
1½ teaspoons salt, optional
  4 cups hot water, divided

Serves 6

Place bacon in 3-qt. casserole; cover. Microwave at High 3 to 5 minutes, or until bacon begins to crisp. Stir in cabbage, onion, seasonings and 2 cups water; cover. Microwave at High 10 minutes. Add remaining water; cover. Microwave at High 8 to 12 minutes, or until cabbage and onions are tender.

NOTE: for low sodium diet omit bacon.

Per Serving:
Calories: 48
Sodium: 547 mg.
Cholesterol: 12 mg.

CHICKEN NOODLE SOUP ▲

2½ to 3 lbs. chicken pieces
  6 cups hot water, divided
  2 large stalks celery, thinly
       sliced
  2 medium carrots, thinly
       sliced
  1 small onion, chopped
 ½ teaspoon dried basil leaves
 ¼ teaspoon rosemary leaves
 ¼ teaspoon poultry seasoning
 ¼ teaspoon pepper
  1 teaspoon salt, optional
 ½ cup thin egg noodles

Serves 8

In 5-qt. casserole combine chicken, 4 cups water, celery, carrots, onion, basil, rosemary, poultry seasoning, pepper and salt; cover. Microwave at High 30 to 40 minutes, or until chicken falls easily from bone, stirring twice during cooking.

Remove chicken from bones. Discard bone and skin. Dice meat

EGG DROP SOUP ▶

4 cups hot water
2 teaspoons instant chicken
    bouillon granules
2 teaspoons soy sauce
1 green onion, chopped
⅛ teaspoon pepper
2 eggs, slightly beaten

Serves 4

In 2-qt. casserole combine water, bouillon, soy sauce, onion and pepper. Microwave at High 7½ to 12 minutes, or until boiling. Pour eggs in a thin circular stream over boiling broth; let threads coagulate. Serve immediately.

NOTE: for low sodium diet substitute low-salt bouillon.

Per Serving:
    Calories: 39
    Sodium: 678 mg.
    Cholesterol: 126 mg.

SPLIT PEA SOUP

4 cups hot water
1 cup green split peas
½ cup chopped onion
½ cup thinly sliced carrots
¼ cup thinly sliced celery
1 tablespoon parsley flakes
½ teaspoon marjoram leaves
½ teaspoon salt, optional
¼ teaspoon thyme leaves
¼ teaspoon basil leaves
⅛ teaspoon pepper

Serves 4

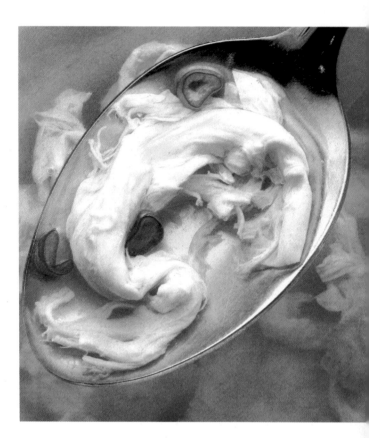

In 3-qt. casserole combine all ingredients. Cover. Microwave at High 8 to 10 minutes, or until boiling. Stir. Reduce power to 50% (Medium). Microwave, covered, 20 to 30 minutes, or until peas are very soft. Remove ¾ to 1 cup peas. Mash thoroughly and stir into soup. Increase power to High. Microwave, uncovered, 10 to 15 minutes, or until mixture is slightly thickened.

Per Serving:
    Calories: 82
    Sodium: 275 mg.
    Cholesterol: 0

ZUCCHINI POCKET SANDWICH ▼

1 cup shredded zucchini
½ cup sliced fresh mushrooms
1 cup chopped tomato
½ teaspoon basil leaves
¼ teaspoon oregano leaves
¼ teaspoon garlic powder
2 tablespoons grated
   Parmesan cheese
4 small loaves pocket bread

Serves 4

In medium mixing bowl combine zucchini and mushrooms. Microwave at High 2 to 3 minutes, or until mushrooms are tender. Drain excess liquid.

Stir in tomato, seasonings and cheese. Split open one end of pocket bread. Place one-fourth of the filling in each.

Per Serving:
  Calories: 114
  Sodium: 140 mg.
  Cholesterol: 8 mg.

VEGIE MELT SANDWICH

1 tablespoon low calorie
    mayonnaise*
½ teaspoon prepared mustard
    Dash dill weed
2 slices firm bread, toasted
2 thin slices red onion
2 thin slices tomato
½ cup alfalfa sprouts
1 slice low fat American
    cheese, cut into 8 strips

Serves 2

In small bowl combine
mayonnaise, mustard and dill
weed. Spread half of mixture on
each slice of toast. Top each with
1 slice onion and tomato, then ¼
cup alfalfa sprouts. Arrange 4
strips cheese over each sandwich.
Place on paper towel-lined plate.
Microwave at 50% (Medium) 1½
to 2½ minutes, or until cheese
melts, rotating once during
cooking.

*40 calories per tablespoon

Per Serving:
  Calories: 118
  Sodium: 280 mg.
  Cholesterol: 3 mg.

MEXICAN PIZZA SANDWICH

2 medium tomatoes, chopped
¼ cup chopped onion
1 tablespoon chopped green
    chili peppers
¼ teaspoon garlic powder
¼ teaspoon ground cumin
½ teaspoon oregano leaves
¼ teaspoon chili powder
    Dash salt
    Dash cayenne pepper
2 slices firm bread, toasted
2 tablespoons shredded
    mozzarella cheese

Serves 2

In 1-qt. casserole combine
tomatoes, onion and chili peppers.
Microwave at High 5 to 6 minutes,
or until tomatoes are tender,
stirring after half the time. Drain.
Stir in seasonings.

Arrange toasted bread in bottom
of 8 × 8-in. baking dish or on
serving dish. Place half of tomato
mixture on each slice. Top each
with 1 tablespoon cheese.
Microwave at High 1 to 2 minutes,
or until cheese melts. Rotate
sandwiches once during cooking.

Per Serving:
  Calories: 134
  Sodium: 150 mg.
  Cholesterol: 9 mg.

EGGS & CHEESE

BAKED CHEESE SANDWICH ▲

8 slices firm white bread
4 slices (¾ oz. each) low fat
   American cheese
2 eggs, slightly beaten
1 cup skim milk
1 tablespoon instant minced
   onion
1 teaspoon prepared mustard
1 teaspoon parsley flakes
   Dash black pepper
⅛ teaspoon cayenne pepper
4 carrot curls, optional

Serves 4

In 8 × 8-in. baking dish place 4 slices bread. Top each slice with a slice of cheese and the remaining bread. In 2-cup measure blend remaining ingredients. Pour slowly over sandwiches. Place plastic wrap directly on sandwich surface. Refrigerate 8 hours or overnight.

Microwave, uncovered, at 50% (Medium) 6 minutes. Rotate each sandwich ½ turn. Microwave 6 to 10 minutes longer, or until sandwiches are set. Garnish with carrot curl, if desired.

NOTE: If desired, 2 eggs may be replaced with ½ cup egg substitute, and a low-sodium cheese product can be substituted for the American cheese.

Per Serving:
  Calories: 285
  Sodium: 485 mg.
  Cholesterol: 134 mg.

QUICHE SUPREME

4 slices firm white bread
1 tablespoon margarine or
　　butter
2 to 3 tablespoons cold water
12 oz. sliced fresh mushrooms
3 eggs, slightly beaten
½ cup evaporated skim milk
⅓ cup chopped green onions
2 teaspoons fresh snipped
　　parsley
¼ teaspoon dry mustard
¼ teaspoon pepper
¼ teaspoon dried oregano
　　leaves

Serves 4

In blender or food processor, chop bread into fine crumbs. Blend in margarine thoroughly. Add enough water to form moist dough. Press dough into pie dish to form crust. Microwave at High 1½ to 2½ minutes, or until sides appear dry. Set aside.

Place mushrooms in 1-qt. casserole. Microwave at High 5 to 7 minutes, or until tender, stirring once or twice. Drain thoroughly. Spread in shell.

In 1-qt. casserole blend eggs and remaining ingredients. Reduce power to 50% (Medium). Microwave 1 minute. Stir mixture. Microwave an additional 1 to 2 minutes, or until hot but not set, stirring every 30 seconds. Pour egg mixture over mushrooms.

Reduce power to 30% (Low). Microwave 7 to 14 minutes, or until soft set, rotating 4 times. Let stand 5 to 10 minutes.

Per Serving:
　Calories:　　195
　Sodium:　　190 mg.
　Cholesterol:　191 mg.

BREAKFAST SOUFFLÉ

1 egg, separated
2 egg whites
½ teaspoon margarine or
　　butter
3 drops yellow food coloring
2 tablespoons skim milk
¼ teaspoon basil leaves
¼ teaspoon salt, optional
⅛ teaspoon curry powder
⅛ teaspoon pepper

Serves 2

Beat 3 egg whites until soft peaks form. In deep cereal bowl microwave margarine at High 30 to 45 seconds, or until melted. Blend food coloring, egg yolk, milk, basil, salt, curry and pepper. Fold into egg whites. Pour into cereal bowl. Reduce power to 50% (Medium).

Microwave 1½ to 3 minutes, or until mixture is set and no liquid can be seen in bottom of dish. Lift edge carefully to check for liquid.

Per Serving:
　Calories:　　78
　Sodium:　　264 mg.
　Cholesterol:　127 mg.

BROCCOLI PROVOLONE OMELET ▼

Open Face Omelet, opposite
½ cup chopped cooked
broccoli, drained
1 oz. Provolone cheese, sliced
into thin strips
Paprika

Serves 4

Prepare Open Face Omelet as directed. Place broccoli on omelet; top with cheese strips. Microwave 1 minute longer, or until cheese melts. Sprinkle with paprika.

Per Serving:
Calories: 120
Sodium: 172 mg.
Cholesterol: 254 mg.

OPEN FACE OMELET

2 teaspoons margarine or
   butter
4 large eggs, separated
¼ teaspoon salt, optional
⅛ teaspoon pepper
   Dash paprika

Serves 4

In 9-in. pie plate melt margarine
at High 30 to 45 seconds; set
aside. In medium bowl beat egg
whites until stiff but not dry. In
small bowl beat yolks lightly. Add
salt, pepper and paprika. Fold
yolk mixture gently into beaten
whites. Pour mixture into pie plate.
Reduce power to 50% (Medium).
Microwave 3 to 5 minutes, or until
partially set. Lift edges to spread
uncooked portions. Microwave
2 to 3 minutes longer, or until
almost set.

Per Serving:
   Calories: 100
   Sodium: 155 mg.
   Cholesterol: 250 mg.

SPICED YOGURT OMELET ▲

   Open Face Omelet, left
¼ cup plain low fat yogurt
⅛ teaspoon ground nutmeg
   Dash ground allspice
½ teaspoon fructose
¼ teaspoon salt, optional

Serves 4

Prepare Open Face Omelet as
directed. Combine yogurt, nutmeg,
allspice, fructose and salt. Spread
mixture over omelet during last
2 to 3 minutes of cooking time.

Per Serving:
   Calories: 113
   Sodium: 155 mg.
   Cholesterol: 250 mg.

ZUCCHINI TOMATO OMELET

   Open Face Omelet, page 63
1 cup shredded zucchini,
    drained
½ cup chopped tomato
2 tablespoons plain low fat
    yogurt
⅛ teaspoon pepper

Serves 4

Prepare Open Face Omelet as directed. Combine remaining ingredients. Spread over omelet during last 1½ to 2 minutes of cooking time.

Per Serving:
Calories: 117
Sodium: 155 mg.
Cholesterol: 250 mg.

SANTA FE SCRAMBLED EGGS

4 large eggs
¼ teaspoon parsley flakes
¼ teaspoon oregano
½ teaspoon salt, optional
⅛ teaspoon basil leaves
    Dash cayenne
¼ cup chopped green pepper
2 green onions, chopped
1 small tomato, chopped
¼ cup shredded mozzarella
    cheese

Serves 4

In medium bowl blend eggs and spices. Stir in chopped green pepper, onions and tomato. Microwave at High 3½ to 4 minutes, or until soft set, stirring 2 or 3 times during cooking.

Stir in mozzarella cheese; cover. Let stand 1 minute, or until cheese melts. Serve immediately.

Per Serving:
Calories: 103
Sodium: 287 mg.
Cholesterol: 255 mg.

CHEESE FONDUE

8 oz. low fat American cheese,
    cut into 1-in. cubes
½ cup skim milk
1 teaspoon dry mustard
2 teaspoons Worcestershire
    sauce
1 teaspoon onion powder
½ teaspoon summer savory
½ teaspoon parsley flakes
2 tablespoons dry sherry

Serves 6

In large mixing bowl combine all ingredients except sherry. Microwave at 50% (Medium) 6 to 8 minutes, or until hot and smooth, stirring 2 or 3 times during cooking. Blend in sherry. Serve warm with raw vegetables.

Per Serving:
Calories: 83
Sodium: 290 mg.
Cholesterol: 14 mg.

CRUSTLESS RICOTTA PIE ▼

   1 pkg. (10 oz.) frozen
       chopped spinach
   ½ cup chopped onion
   2 eggs
1½ cups ricotta cheese
   ¼ teaspoon salt, optional
   ¼ teaspoon pepper
   ¼ teaspoon dried dill weed
   ⅛ teaspoon garlic powder
   2 teaspoons all-purpose flour
   ⅛ teaspoon paprika

Serves 8

Combine spinach and onion in
1½-qt. casserole; cover. Microwave
at High 4 to 6 minutes, stirring
after half the time. Drain well.

In medium mixing bowl beat eggs
with fork. Stir in ricotta, salt,
pepper, dill, garlic powder and
flour. Blend in spinach and onion.
Spread spinach mixture in 9-in.
pie plate with rubber spatula.
Sprinkle with paprika.

Microwave at High 4 minutes,
rotating every 2 minutes. Reduce
power to 50% (Medium).
Microwave 3 to 11 minutes longer,
or until center is set. Let stand
5 minutes.

Per Serving:
   Calories: 61
   Sodium: 100 mg.
   Cholesterol: 66 mg.

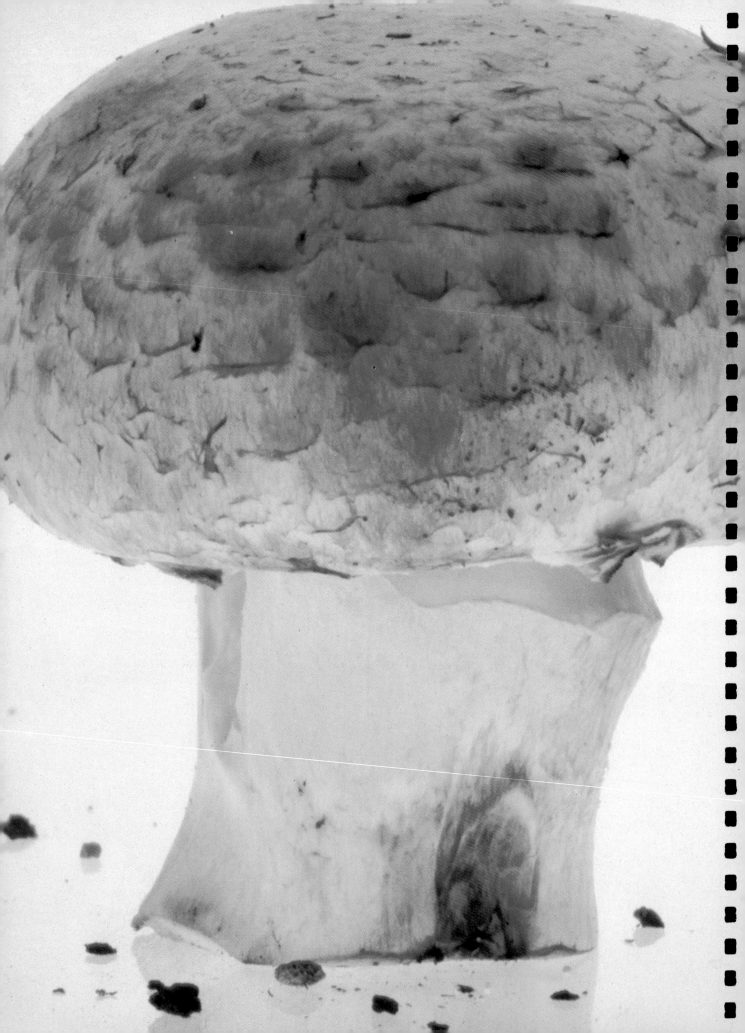

VEGETABLES & FRUITS

DILLED GREEN BEANS

1 pkg. (10 oz.) frozen cut
  green beans
2 tablespoons water
2 green onions, finely
  chopped
2 teaspoons cornstarch
½ cup water
¼ teaspoon dill weed
  Dash pepper
1 teaspoon cider vinegar
1 teaspoon instant chicken
  bouillon granules
¼ teaspoon grated lime peel

Serves 4

Place beans and 2 tablespoons
water in 1-qt. casserole; cover.
Microwave at High 4 to 7 minutes,
or until beans are tender, stirring
to break apart after half the time.
Drain. Cover and set aside.

In small bowl or 2-cup measure
blend remaining ingredients.
Microwave at High 1½ to 2 minutes, or until clear and thickened.
Pour over beans. Toss to coat.

NOTE: for low sodium diet
substitute low-salt bouillon.

Per Serving:
  Calories: 38
  Sodium: 136 mg.
  Cholesterol: 0

CRUNCHY ASPARAGUS ▶

1 pkg. (10 oz.) frozen
  asparagus cuts
2 tablespoons water
1 teaspoon lemon juice
3 to 4 drops red pepper sauce
⅛ teaspoon pepper
¼ teaspoon salt, optional
¼ teaspoon basil leaves
1 tablespoon sunflower nuts
  Lemon slices

Serves 4

Place asparagus and water in 1-qt.
casserole; cover. Microwave at
High 4½ to 5½ minutes, or until
asparagus is hot, stirring after half
the cooking time to break apart.
Drain. Cover and set aside.

In small bowl or 1-cup measure
combine lemon juice, red pepper
sauce and seasonings. Pour
mixture over asparagus. Toss to
coat. Sprinkle with sunflower
nuts. Garnish with lemon slices
if desired.

Per Serving:
  Calories: 32
  Sodium: 145 mg.
  Cholesterol: 0

BROCCOLI & CAULIFLOWER WITH MUSTARD SAUCE ▼

   2 cups fresh broccoli
       flowerets
   2 cups fresh cauliflowerets
   ⅓ to ½ cup skim milk
   1 tablespoon all-purpose flour
1½ teaspoons prepared
       mustard
   ¼ teaspoon salt, optional
       Dash garlic powder
       Dash white pepper

Serves 4

Combine broccoli and cauliflower in baking dish. Cover. Microwave at High 8 to 11 minutes, or until tender, stirring once. Drain; set vegetables aside.

In medium bowl blend remaining ingredients with wire whip. Microwave at High 2 to 3 minutes, or until thickened, stirring every minute. Pour over vegetables. Toss to coat.

Per Serving:
Calories: 50
Sodium: 166 mg.
Cholesterol: 0

ITALIAN BROCCOLI WITH TOMATOES

4 cups fresh broccoli flowerets
½ cup water
½ teaspoon Italian seasoning
½ teaspoon dried parsley flakes
¼ teaspoon salt, optional
⅛ teaspoon pepper
2 medium tomatoes, cut into wedges
½ cup shredded mozzarella cheese

Serves 6

Place broccoli and water in 2-qt. casserole; cover. Microwave at High 5 to 8 minutes, or until tender-crisp. Drain. Stir in seasonings and tomatoes. Microwave, uncovered, at High 2 to 4 minutes, or until tomatoes are hot. Sprinkle with mozzarella. Microwave 1 minute, or until cheese melts.

Per Serving:
Calories: 67
Sodium: 107 mg.
Cholesterol: 6 mg.

LEMON BRUSSELS SPROUTS

1 pkg. (10 oz.) frozen Brussels sprouts
1 tablespoon water
½ teaspoon lemon juice
¼ teaspoon grated lemon peel
Dash pepper
Dash ground thyme

Serves 4

In 1-qt. casserole combine Brussels sprouts, water, lemon juice and lemon peel; cover. Microwave at High 3 minutes. Stir to break apart; re-cover. Microwave at High 2 to 3 minutes, or until Brussels sprouts are tender. Drain; sprinkle with seasonings.

Per Serving:
Calories: 25
Sodium: 63 mg.
Cholesterol: 0

HARVARD BEETS

2 teaspoons cornstarch
¼ teaspoon salt, optional
Dash pepper
Dash ground allspice
¼ teaspoon grated orange peel
2 tablespoons cider vinegar
1 can (16 oz.) sliced beets, drained, ⅓ cup liquid reserved
1 tablespoon orange juice

Serves 4

In 1-qt. casserole combine cornstarch, salt, pepper, allspice and orange peel. Blend in vinegar, beet liquid and orange juice.

Microwave at High 1¾ to 2½ minutes, or until clear and thickened, stirring every minute. Add beets. Microwave at High 1 to 4 minutes, or until beets are thoroughly heated.

Per Serving:
Calories: 40
Sodium: 172 mg.
Cholesterol: 0

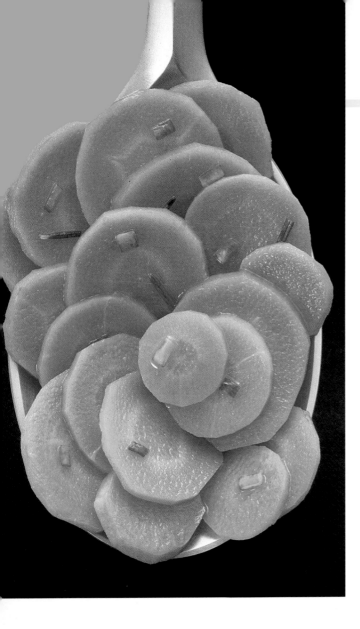

NOTE: for low sodium diet
substitute low-salt bouillon.

Per Serving:
Calories: 65
Sodium: 235 mg.
Cholesterol: 0

CARROT MEDLEY

4 cups thinly sliced carrots
1 small onion, sliced and
      separated into rings
2 teaspoons fresh, chopped
      parsley
1 teaspoon sugar
1 tablespoon margarine or
      butter
1 teaspoon instant chicken
      bouillon granules
   Paprika

Serves 6

Combine all ingredients in 2-qt.
casserole; cover. Microwave at
High 7 to 10 minutes, or until
carrots are tender-crisp, stirring
after half the cooking time.
Sprinkle with paprika.

NOTE: for low sodium diet
substitute low-salt bouillon.

Per Serving:
Calories: 68
Sodium: 215 mg.
Cholesterol: 0

ROSEMARY CARROTS ▲

2 cups thinly sliced carrots
1 teaspoon instant chicken
      bouillon granules
2 tablespoons hot water
1 tablespoon brown sugar
¼ teaspoon dried rosemary,
      crushed
1 tablespoon chopped chives
⅛ teaspoon white pepper

Serves 4

Place carrots in 2-qt. casserole.
In small bowl or 2-cup measure
combine bouillon, water, sugar
and seasonings. Pour over carrots.
Toss to coat; cover. Microwave at
High 5 to 8 minutes, or until fork
tender, stirring once after half the
cooking time.

ZUCCHINI WITH PIMIENTO ▼

2 cups thinly sliced zucchini
   (2 medium)
1 jar (2 oz.) pimiento, drained
   and diced
½ teaspoon salt, optional
½ teaspoon oregano leaves
1 small onion, chopped
⅛ teaspoon garlic powder
⅛ teaspoon cayenne

Serves 4

In 2-qt. casserole mix together all
ingredients; cover. Microwave at
High 6 to 7 minutes, or until fork
tender, stirring once.

Per Serving:
  Calories: 25
  Sodium: 254 mg.
  Cholesterol: 0

High 7 to 10 minutes, or until eggplant is translucent, stirring 2 or 3 times.

Per Serving:
Calories: 33
Sodium: 105 mg.
Cholesterol: 3 mg.

RATATOUILLE ▲

½ lb. eggplant, cut into
   ½-in. cubes
⅛ teaspoon instant minced
   garlic
1 small onion, sliced and
   separated into rings
1 small zucchini, thinly sliced
½ medium green pepper,
   chopped
1 stalk celery, chopped
1 tomato, cut into wedges
   Dash pepper
¼ teaspoon salt, optional
¼ teaspoon chervil leaves
¼ teaspoon oregano leaves
⅛ teaspoon thyme leaves
1 tablespoon grated Parmesan
   cheese

Serves 6

Combine all ingredients in 2-qt. casserole; cover. Microwave at

BRAISED ONIONS WITH TOMATOES

¼ cup hot water
1 teaspoon instant beef
   bouillon granules
2 tablespoons white wine
1 teaspoon snipped fresh
   parsley
¼ teaspoon dry mustard
⅛ teaspoon pepper
2 large white onions, sliced
   and separated into rings
1 small tomato, cut into
   8 wedges

Serves 4

In 1-cup measure combine hot water, bouillon, wine and seasonings. Place onion rings in 2-qt. casserole. Pour bouillon mixture over onions. Toss to coat; cover. Microwave at High 5 to 7 minutes, or until onions are tender, stirring after half the cooking time. Stir in tomato. Microwave at High 1 minute.

NOTE: for low sodium diet substitute low-salt bouillon.

Per Serving:
Calories: 21
Sodium: 241 mg.
Cholesterol: 0

HAM POTATO TOPPER ▶

    4 medium baking potatoes
    ¼ cup skim milk
    2 tablespoons plain low fat
        yogurt
    ¼ cup hot water
    ½ teaspoon salt, optional
    ⅛ teaspoon pepper
    ¼ teaspoon onion powder
    1 teaspoon freeze-dried
        chives
    3½ oz. canned chunk ham
        Paprika

Serves 8

Bake potatoes as directed, opposite. Halve each baked potato lengthwise. Scoop out centers, leaving ¼-in. shell. Set shells aside. In medium mixing bowl combine potato, milk, yogurt, water, salt, pepper, onion powder and chives. Beat until smooth and fluffy. Flake ham. Gently stir into potato mixture.

Pipe or spoon potato mixture into shells. Sprinkle with paprika. Arrange in 12 × 8-in. baking dish. Microwave at High 4½ to 6 minutes, or until thoroughly heated.

    Per Serving:
    Calories: 124
    Sodium: 360 mg.
    Cholesterol: 18 mg.

BAKED POTATOES

4 medium baking potatoes

Serves 4

Prick well-scrubbed potatoes twice with fork. Arrange 1 inch apart on paper towel on oven floor. Microwave at High 10½ to 12½ minutes, turning over and rearranging after half the time. Potatoes will feel slightly firm. Wrap in foil; let stand 5 to 10 minutes to complete cooking.

    Per Serving:
    Calories: 70
    Sodium: 0
    Cholesterol: 0

FRUITED CHEESE DANISH

2 eggs, slightly beaten
2 tablespoons skim milk
¾ teaspoon cinnamon, divided
½ teaspoon vanilla extract
4 slices firm white bread
2 teaspoons margarine or
   butter
⅛ teaspoon ground nutmeg
½ cup cream style cottage
   cheese
1 cup sliced fresh strawberries

Serves 4

In shallow bowl blend eggs, milk,
½ teaspoon cinnamon and vanilla.
Soak bread in egg mixture. Place
bread on wax paper. Preheat
10-in. browning dish at High 5
minutes. Immediately add margarine and bread. Microwave
at High 1 minute. Turn slices over.
Microwave at High 2 to 4 minutes,
or until bread is dry to the touch.
Blend remaining cinnamon and
nutmeg with cottage cheese.
Spoon one-fourth cottage cheese
on each bread slice. Microwave at
High 1 minute to melt cheese. Top
each with ¼ cup sliced fresh
strawberries.

Per Serving:
   Calories: 180
   Sodium: 232 mg.
   Cholesterol: 131 mg.

BAKED GRAPEFRUIT

2 grapefruit
8 teaspoons low sugar
   strawberry spread
4 whole fresh strawberries

Serves 4

Cut grapefruit in half. Loosen
each section. Top halves with
strawberry spread.

Microwave at High 4 to 6 minutes,
or until grapefruit are very hot,
rotating after half the time. Top
each half with a fresh strawberry
in the center.

Per Serving:
   Calories: 62
   Sodium: 0
   Cholesterol: 0

APPLE TOPPING

4 cups diced apples
2 tablespoons fructose
½ teaspoon ground cinnamon
¼ teaspoon ground nutmeg
¼ teaspoon ground ginger

Serves 8

Stir all ingredients together in
2-qt. casserole. Microwave at High
4 to 6 minutes, or until apples are
tender, stirring once or twice.
Serve warm or cold, over toast or
hot cereal.

Per Serving:
   Calories: 40
   Sodium: 1 mg.
   Cholesterol: 0

STRAWBERRY RHUBARB ▲ COMPOTE

- 4 cups (20 oz. pkg.) frozen rhubarb, cut into 1-in. pieces
- ¼ teaspoon cinnamon Dash ground cloves
- ¼ cup water
- 2 cups sliced fresh strawberries
- ¼ cup fructose
- 5 to 7 drops red food coloring

Serves 6

In 2-qt. casserole combine rhubarb, cinnamon, cloves and water; cover. Microwave at High 10 to 14 minutes, or until rhubarb is tender, stirring 2 or 3 times. Mash rhubarb slightly. Stir in strawberries, fructose and food coloring.

Reduce power to 50% (Medium). Microwave 1 minute, or until strawberries are heated. For a sweeter compote, serve chilled.

Per Serving:
Calories: 65
Sodium: 16 mg.
Cholesterol: 0

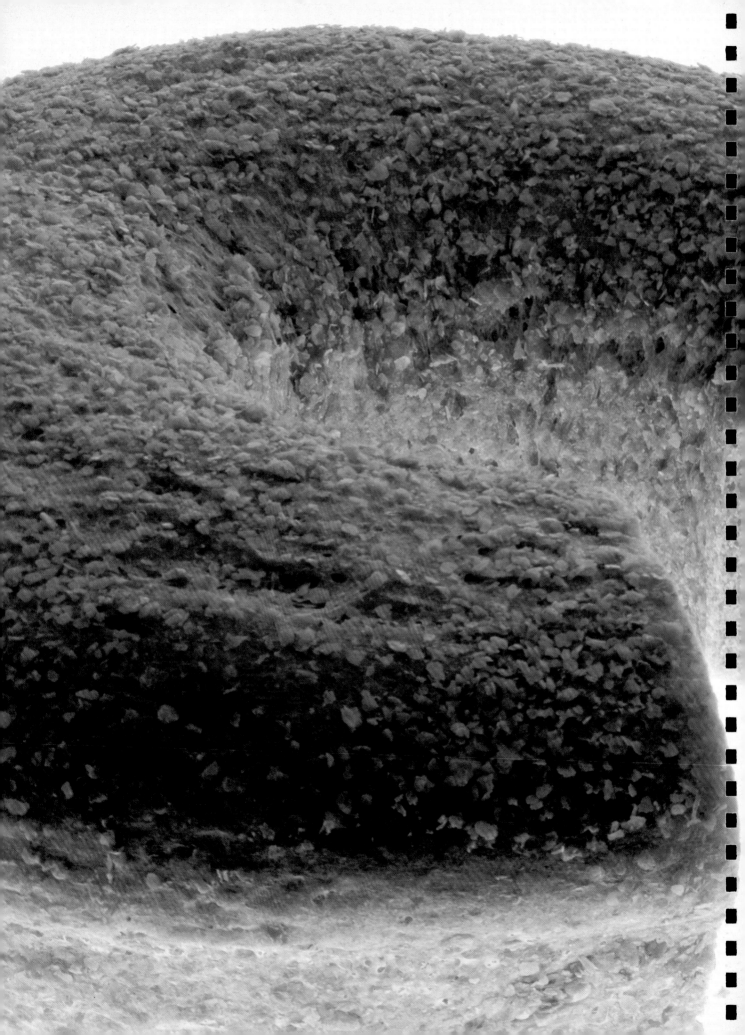

BREADS &
DESSERTS

◄CHEWY WHEAT LOAF

1 tablespoon lemon juice
 Skim milk
1 cup whole wheat flour
¼ cup brown sugar
1 teaspoon baking powder
1 teaspoon baking soda
¼ cup vegetable oil
2 eggs, slightly beaten
1 teaspoon apple pie spice
⅛ teaspoon nutmeg

Makes 18 slices
Serving size: 1 slice

In 1-cup measure combine lemon juice and enough milk to equal ½ cup. Stir.

Combine all remaining ingredients in medium mixing bowl. Stir in milk and lemon juice. Beat at low speed of electric mixer 1 minute. Line 9×5-in. loaf dish with wax paper cut to fit bottom. Add batter. Shield ends of loaf with 2½-in. wide strips of aluminum foil, covering batter with 1½ inches and molding remainder around handles of dish.

Microwave at 50% (Medium) 5 minutes, rotating dish once or twice. Increase power to High.

Microwave 1½ to 4 minutes, or until top of bread is firm to touch and almost dry, with a little moisture still visible. No uncooked batter should be visible through bottom of dish.

Let stand 3 minutes. Turn out of pan. Cut into 18 slices.

Per Serving:
 Calories: 88
 Sodium: 80 mg.
 Cholesterol: 28 mg.

RAISIN ORANGE MUFFINS

½ cup rolled oats
1 cup whole wheat flour
2 tablespoons vegetable oil
¼ cup sugar
2 teaspoons baking powder
¼ teaspoon salt
⅔ cup skim milk
2 eggs, slightly beaten
¼ cup raisins
1 teaspoon grated orange peel
¼ teaspoon ground allspice

Makes 12 muffins
Serving size: 1 muffin

Combine all ingredients in large mixing bowl. Stir just until particles are moistened. Line each muffin or custard cup with two paper liners; fill half full. Microwave at High as directed below, or until top springs back when touched, rotating and rearranging after half the time.

1 muffin	¼ to ¾ minute
2 muffins	½ to 2 minutes
4 muffins	1 to 2½ minutes
6 muffins	2 to 4½ minutes

Per Serving:
 Calories: 113
 Sodium: 100 mg.
 Cholesterol: 42 mg.

CARROT BRAN MUFFINS

1 cup 40% bran flakes
¾ cup skim milk
2 cups finely shredded carrot
1 cup whole wheat flour
2 tablespoons brown sugar
2 tablespoons vegetable oil
1 tablespoon lemon juice
1 teaspoon baking powder
½ teaspoon baking soda
½ teaspoon pumpkin pie spice
¼ teaspoon salt
1 egg, slightly beaten

Makes 14 muffins
Serving size: 1 muffin

Combine bran, milk and carrot; let stand 5 minutes. Add remaining ingredients, stirring until particles are moistened. Line each muffin or custard cup with two paper liners; fill half full. Microwave at High as directed below, or until top springs back when touched, rotating and rearranging after half the time.

1 muffin	¼ to ¾ minute
2 muffins	½ to 2 minutes
4 muffins	1 to 2½ minutes
6 muffins	2 to 4½ minutes

Per Serving:
Calories: 86
Sodium: 87 mg.
Cholesterol: 18 mg.

WHEAT BISCUITS ▶

½ cup whole wheat flour
1 cup all-purpose white flour
2½ teaspoons baking powder
¼ teaspoon salt
3 tablespoons margarine or
    butter
½ cup skim milk
¾ teaspoon poppy seeds
1 tablespoon wheat germ

Makes 10 biscuits
Serving size: 1 biscuit

In medium mixing bowl combine flour, baking powder and salt. Cut in margarine until particles are fine. Add milk and stir until dough clings together.

Knead on lightly floured surface 12 times. Pat out to ¾-in. thickness. Top with poppy seed and wheat germ. Cut into 1½-in. circles. Place biscuits ½ inch apart on paper towels. Microwave at High 1½ to 2 minutes, or until dry and puffy, rotating ¼ turn every 30 seconds.

Per Serving:
Calories: 100
Sodium: 164 mg.
Cholesterol: 0

LEMON CHEESECAKE

1 pkg. (8 oz.) Neufchâtel
   cheese
1 tablespoon fresh lemon juice
1 tablespoon grated lemon
   peel
2 eggs
¼ cup fructose
1 teaspoon graham cracker
   crumbs
⅛ teaspoon ground mace

Serves 6

In medium mixing bowl microwave cheese at 50% (Medium) 1 to 2 minutes, or until softened. Add lemon juice, peel, eggs and fructose. Beat at medium speed of electric mixer 2 minutes, or until well blended.

Pour into 9 × 5-in. loaf dish. Sprinkle graham cracker crumbs and mace on top. Shield ends of dish with 2-in. wide strips of foil.

Microwave at 50% (Medium) 5 to 11 minutes, or until center is soft set, turning ¼ turn every 2 minutes. Cool to room temperature. Refrigerate until well chilled.

Per Serving:
Calories: 177
Sodium: 39 mg.
Cholesterol: 155 mg.

LEMON-LIME SOUFFLÉ

1 cup diet lemon-lime soda
2 tablespoons cornstarch
1 tablespoon lime juice
1 teaspoon grated lemon peel
1 teaspoon grated lime peel
1 tablespoon fructose
2 to 4 drops green food
   coloring
1 egg yolk
3 egg whites
   Lime slice, optional

Serves 4

In small bowl or 2-cup measure combine diet soda, cornstarch, lime juice, lemon and lime peel, fructose and food coloring. Microwave at High 2½ to 3 minutes, or until thickened, stirring 2 or 3 times.

Beat egg yolk in small bowl. Stir 1 tablespoon of hot lemon-lime mixture into egg yolk; blend egg yolk mixture back into hot lemon-lime mixture. Set aside.

In medium bowl whip egg whites until soft peaks form. Fold lemon-lime mixture gently into whites. Pour into 1-qt. casserole. Reduce power to 30% (Low). Microwave 9 to 12 minutes, or until set, rotating ¼ turn every 2 minutes. Serve immediately. Garnish with lime slice, if desired.

Per Serving:
Calories: 61
Sodium: 46 mg.
Cholesterol: 69 mg.

TROPICAL CHIFFON

2 cans (8 oz. each) crushed
    pineapple, packed in own
    juice, drained, juice reserved
1 teaspoon grated orange peel
    Water
1 tablespoon unflavored gelatin
2 eggs, separated
2 kiwi fruit, peeled, sliced into
    eighths

Serves 8

Measure pineapple juice into medium mixing bowl. Add grated orange peel. Add enough water to equal 1¼ cups. Stir in gelatin. Microwave at High 1 minute, stirring to dissolve gelatin.

Beat egg yolks slightly. Stir in small amount of warm gelatin mixture. Blend back into the remaining gelatin.

Reduce power to 50% (Medium). Microwave 30 to 60 seconds, or until the yolk mixture thickens slightly, stirring once. Refrigerate until soft set.

In medium mixing bowl beat egg whites until stiff peaks form. Beat yolk mixture until smooth; gently fold into egg whites.

Divide pineapple into 8 custard cups or small bowls. Cut kiwi fruit slices into quarters. Arrange 7 quarters of the kiwi fruit over the pineapple in each cup.

Top with the egg white mixture. Garnish each with one quarter of kiwi fruit. Chill before serving.

Per Serving:
Calories:	76
Sodium:	15 mg.
Cholesterol:	69 mg.

BAKED APPLES

4 medium apples
⅓ cup diet cream soda
½ teaspoon rum extract
¼ teaspoon cinnamon
⅛ teaspoon ginger

Serves 4

Core apples, leaving ½ inch of bottom intact. Place in custard cups. Combine soda, rum extract and spices in 1-cup measure. Spoon mixture into centers of apples. Cover each apple loosely with plastic wrap. Microwave at High 4 to 5½ minutes, or until apples are fork tender, rearranging and rotating apples after half the cooking time. Let stand 2 minutes. Serve warm.

Per Serving:
Calories:	88
Sodium:	7 mg.
Cholesterol:	0

◄ APPLE CRÊPES

8 crêpes, page 88
¼ cup orange juice
1 teaspoon cornstarch
⅛ teaspoon ground cloves
2 cups unpeeled, chopped apples, ¼-in. pieces
2 tablespoons vanilla low fat yogurt
⅛ teaspoon orange extract

Serves 8

In 1-qt. casserole combine orange juice, cornstarch and cloves. Stir in apples; cover. Microwave at High 7 to 9 minutes, or until apples soften and sauce thickens, stirring once or twice. Place 3 tablespoons mixture on each crêpe; roll up around filling. In small bowl combine yogurt and extract. Top each crêpe with ¾ teaspoon mixture.

Per Serving:
Calories: 49
Sodium: 25 mg.
Cholesterol: 15 mg.

BANANA CRÊPES►

8 crêpes, page 88
1 cup diet cream soda
2 teaspoons cornstarch
¼ teaspoon ground ginger
1 teaspoon cinnamon
3 ripe bananas, cut into ½-in. chunks
¼ cup vanilla low fat yogurt
Dash cinnamon
Dash nutmeg

Serves 8

In 1-qt. casserole blend soda, cornstarch, ginger and 1 teaspoon cinnamon. Stir in bananas. Microwave at High 3½ to 6½ minutes, or until thickened, stirring 2 or 3 times.

Place 3 tablespoons of banana mixture on each crêpe; roll up around filling.

In small bowl blend yogurt, dash of cinnamon and dash of nutmeg. Top each crêpe with 1½ teaspoons of yogurt mixture.

Per Serving:
Calories: 91
Sodium: 29 mg.
Cholesterol: 15 mg.

CRÊPES

1 cup all-purpose flour
1½ cups skim milk
1 egg, slightly beaten
¼ teaspoon salt, optional
   Vegetable oil

Makes 18 crêpes

Blend flour, milk, egg, and salt. Heat lightly oiled 6-in. skillet on conventional range. Pour 2 tablespoons batter in skillet; cook until golden brown on bottom. Turn over. Brown other side. Repeat with remaining batter. Use in one of the crêpe recipes on page 88.

NOTE: Leftover crêpes may be frozen between 2 layers of wax paper.

Per Serving:
Calories: 31
Sodium: 25 mg.
Cholesterol: 15 mg.

GINGER PEACH PARFAIT ▶

1 pkg. (1⅔ oz.) low calorie
   vanilla pudding mix
1½ cups skim milk
1 cup drained, chopped
   peaches
¼ teaspoon cinnamon
⅜ teaspoon ground ginger
1 cup prepared low calorie
   whipped topping

Serves 4

In medium bowl blend pudding mix and milk. Microwave at High 4 to 6 minutes, or until slightly thickened, stirring 2 or 3 times during cooking. Stir in peaches. Cover with plastic wrap. Chill until set.

Blend spices into whipped topping. In each of 4 parfait glasses layer ¼ cup chilled pudding mix, 3 tablespoons whipped topping, ¼ cup pudding and 1 tablespoon topping.

Per Serving:
Calories: 163
Sodium: 64 mg.
Cholesterol: 0

ORANGE FRUIT BAKE

2 large bananas, halved
   lengthwise, cut into 1-in.
   pieces
2 large oranges, peeled and
   sectioned
¼ cup green grapes, halved
¼ cup orange juice
¼ teaspoon rum extract
1 tablespoon water
¼ teaspoon grated orange rind
2 teaspoons brown sugar

Serves 4

Divide fruit evenly into 4 custard cups. Set aside. Combine orange juice, rum extract, water and orange rind in 1-cup measure. Microwave at High 1 to 1½ minutes, or until boiling. Pour sauce over fruit in custard cups; stir to coat fruit. Sprinkle each fruit cup with ½ teaspoon brown sugar. Let stand 10 minutes. Cover with wax paper.

Microwave at High 2 to 2½ minutes, or until bananas begin to soften, rotating once during cooking. Serve warm.

Per Serving:
   Calories: 123
   Sodium: 2 mg.
   Cholesterol: 0

PEACH MELBA

1 can (16 oz.) peach halves
   in light syrup, drained
½ cup low sugar raspberry jam
1 cup prepared low calorie
   whipped topping

Serves 4

Arrange peaches in 12 × 8-in. baking dish. Cover with plastic wrap. Microwave at High 1 to 2 minutes, or until warm, rearranging after half the time.

Microwave jam in 1-cup measure at High 30 to 60 seconds, or until thinned, stirring once. Place peach halves in 4 serving dishes. Top each with ¼ cup whipped topping, then 2 tablespoons jam. Serve immediately.

Per Serving:
   Calories: 92
   Sodium: 16 mg.
   Cholesterol: 0

CHOCOLATE CREAM MOUSSE

  1 envelope (1 oz.) low
    calorie chocolate
    pudding mix
1½ cups skim milk
  ¼ teaspoon orange extract
  ½ teaspoon butter flavoring
  1 egg white
  2 teaspoons fructose
  4 tablespoons prepared low
    calorie whipped topping

Serves 4

In small mixing bowl combine pudding mix and milk. Microwave at High 5 to 7 minutes, or until slightly thickened, stirring 2 or 3 times. Stir in orange extract and butter flavoring. Cover top of pudding with wax paper. Let cool.

In small bowl combine egg white and fructose. Whip until egg whites form stiff peaks. Fold in pudding. Spoon into serving dishes; chill. To serve, top with 1 tablespoon whipped topping.

Per Serving:
Calories: 97
Sodium: 65 mg.
Cholesterol: 0

EGG CUSTARD

  3 eggs
  2 tablespoons fructose
  ½ teaspoon vanilla
  ¼ teaspoon salt, optional
  ¼ teaspoon nutmeg, divided
  ½ cup skim milk
  ¼ cup water

Serves 6

In small bowl beat eggs, fructose, vanilla, salt and ⅛ teaspoon nutmeg until smooth. Set aside.

Combine milk and water in 2-cup measure. Microwave at High 1½ to 2 minutes, or until mixture is hot but not boiling. Stir in egg mixture until smooth. Pour into individual custard cups. Top with remaining nutmeg. Reduce power to 50% (Medium). Microwave 3½ to 4½ minutes, or until soft set, turning and rearranging every 30 seconds. Serve chilled.

Per Serving:
Calories: 57
Sodium: 71 mg.
Cholesterol: 138 mg.

AUTUMN PUDDING

1 pkg. (12 oz.) frozen cooked
   squash
1 tablespoon brown sugar
1 teaspoon pumpkin pie spice
1 egg, slightly beaten
½ cup buttermilk
2 tablespoons prepared low
   calorie whipped topping

Serves 4

Place squash in 1-qt. casserole.
Microwave at High 4 minutes, or
until defrosted, stirring to break
apart. Stir in sugar and spice.
Microwave at High 2 minutes,
or until very hot, stirring once.

In small bowl combine egg and
buttermilk. Add a small amount
of hot squash. Stir back into
remaining squash. Reduce power
to 50% (Medium). Microwave 3½
to 4½ minutes, or until slightly
thickened, stirring 2 or 3 times.
Place ⅓ cup of the mixture into
each custard cup. Chill to set.
Chill remaining squash mixture,
then combine with whipped
topping. Divide evenly between
custard cups. Chill.

Per Serving:
  Calories: 100
  Sodium: 58 mg.
  Cholesterol: 72 mg.

CHOCOLATE ALMOND TAPIOCA PUDDING

2 pkgs. (¾ oz. each) low
   calorie instant hot cocoa mix
1¼ cups water
2 tablespoons quick-cooking
   tapioca
2 teaspoons fructose
¼ teaspoon almond extract
2 eggs, separated
⅛ teaspoon cream of tartar

Serves 6

In medium bowl combine all
ingredients except egg whites and
cream of tartar. Beat with a wire
whip. Microwave at High 3½ to
5½ minutes, or until boiling,
stirring once or twice. Boil 1
minute. Cool mixture to room
temperature. Set aside.

Beat egg whites with cream of
tartar until soft peaks form. Fold
egg whites into tapioca mixture.
Serve immediately or chill.

Per Serving:
  Calories: 112
  Sodium: 56 mg.
  Cholesterol: 85 mg.

BAKED PEARS ▲

  2 fresh Bartlett pears
 ¼ cup orange juice
  1 tablespoon raisins or
       currants
 ¼ teaspoon grated lemon peel
  1 teaspoon cornstarch
 ¼ cup water
       Dash allspice
 ⅛ teaspoon cinnamon

Serves 4

Cut pears in half lengthwise; core.
Pierce inside of pear halves with
fork. Arrange cut side up in
8 × 8-in. baking dish.

In 2-cup measure combine
orange juice, raisins, lemon peel,
cornstarch, water, allspice and
cinnamon. Microwave at High 1
to 3 minutes, or until thickened,
stirring once or twice. Pour the
glaze over pear halves. Cover with
wax paper.

Microwave at High 4 to 6 minutes,
or until tender, rearranging and
basting with glaze once during
cooking. Let stand 5 minutes.
Serve warm with remaining glaze.

Per Serving:
Calories: 53
Sodium: 0
Cholesterol: 0

94

INDEX